PROGRESSIVE FILING

PROGRESSIVE

JEFFREY R. STEWART, JR., Ed.D.
Professor of Business Education
Virginia Polytechnic Institute
and State University
Blacksburg, Virginia

JUDITH A. SCHARLE, M.S.
Adult Education Specialist
Norfolk Public Schools
Norfolk, Virginia

GILBERT KAHN, Ed.D.
Late Professor of Business Education
Montclair State College
Upper Montclair, New Jersey

GREGG DIVISION/McGRAW-HILL BOOK COMPANY
New York   Atlanta   Dallas   St. Louis   San Francisco   Auckland   Bogotá
Düsseldorf   Johannesburg   London   Madrid   Mexico   Montreal   New Delhi
Panama   Paris   São Paulo   Singapore   Sydney   Tokyo   Toronto

FILING
NINTH EDITION

Sponsoring Editor	Ella Pezzuti
Editing Supervisor	Timothy Perrin
Production Supervisor	Priscilla Taguer
Design Supervisor	Nancy Ovedovitz
Art Supervisor	Howard Brotman
Cover and Interior Designer	Jorge Hernandez-Porto
Technical Studio	Burmar Technical Corp.

Library of Congress Cataloging in Publication Data

Stewart, Jeffrey Robert, date
  Progressive filing.

  Authors' names in reverse order in previous ed.
  Includes index.
  1. Indexing. 2. Files and filing (Documents)
I. Scharle, Judith A., date, joint author.
II. Kahn, Gilbert, date, joint author.
III. Kahn, Gilbert, date. Progressive
filing. IV. Title.
HF5736.K28 1980   651.5   79-26178
ISBN 0-07-061445-8

   4 5 6 7 8 9 0 DODO 8 9 8 7 6 5 4 3 2

Preface

Progressive Filing, Ninth Edition, treats the major filing and records management competencies needed for entry-level employment in a wide range of office occupations. Whether the student will be employed in a secretarial, stenographic, typing, accounting, word processing, data processing, or records management occupation, the skills and information needed to deal with the paperwork associated with these jobs are presented in this book. Specific competencies are listed at the beginning of each chapter (including competencies correlated with the *Practice Set for Progressive Filing, Ninth Edition*). Reference is made to each competency in the chapter, and practice on each competency is provided within or at the end of each chapter. It is therefore easy for both student and teacher to select those competencies that will be most applicable to the office position sought by the student and to tailor the filing course to the student's needs.

Features

The ninth edition retains many of the features of the previous edition and includes several new elements that take into account the changes in office technology and procedures.

Structured Presentation of Indexing Rules.   The newly revised indexing rules are now treated in two chapters. Chapter 2 presents the indexing rules that deal with names of individuals; Chapter 3 covers the rules that apply to business and organization names. The presentation of the rules is structured so that the student receives practice on a few rules at a time and progresses from the less complex rules to those that are more complex.

Liberal Use of Illustrations.   A hallmark of *Progressive Filing* for many years has been its visual approach to filing. The ninth edition, too, provides many illustrations of forms, systems, steps, supplies, and equipment.

New Treatment of Work Station Organization.   An entirely new chapter is devoted to the organization of the employee's work station on the job. Chapter 7 deals with the arrangement of the desk top and desk drawers, as well as with forms files, log books, reference books for the desk, priority setting, follow-up files, and setting up new files at the work station. All these topics represent significant filing and records management activities for most office workers.

Correlated Practice Set.   A completely new practice set has been developed for, and is correlated with, *Progressive Filing, Ninth Edition.* The *Practice Set for Progressive Filing, Ninth Edition,* contains guides and hanging folders for the seven most-used filing systems: (1) alphabetic card, (2) alphabetic correspondence, (3) alphabetic subject correspondence, (4) numeric subject correspondence, (5) consecutive numeric card, (6) terminal-digit card, and (7) geographic card. In addition, the set provides practice in preparing file labels, cross-referencing, organizing letters chronologically for follow-up, charging out letters, transferring letters from active to inactive status, and filing correspondence geographically. The set includes all the cards, letters, answer sheets, and other forms needed to complete the jobs in the set. The *Practice Set* also includes comprehensive performance and objective tests.

Supporting Materials

The following publications are available and may be used to supplement *Progressive Filing, Ninth Edition,* and the *Practice Set for Progressive Filing.*

Gregg Filing Transparencies, Volume I: Alphabetic Indexing, presents the 25 indexing rules as well as illustrated instructions for steps in card filing, typing captions on file cards, and cross-referencing in card files.

Gregg Filing Transparencies, Volume II: Systems and Procedures, contains illustrations and teacher's guide notes on filing systems and procedures, including alphabetic, numeric, subject, and geographic.

Workbook Exercises in Alphabetic Filing, Third Edition, provides file cards containing over 650 names for extensive practice in the application of the 25 indexing rules.

Teacher's Manual and Key for Progressive Filing, Ninth Edition, includes teaching suggestions, alternate time schedules, and a complete key to *Progressive Filing, Ninth Edition,* the *Practice Set for Progressive Filing,* and the tests included in the *Practice Set.* The objective tests in the *Practice Set* are also printed in the *Teacher's Manual* so that teachers who do not have the *Practice Set* may reproduce them for their classes.

Acknowledgment

The authors appreciate the constructive ideas and suggestions received from the many users of the previous editions of *Progressive Filing.*

Jeffrey R. Stewart, Jr.
Judith A. Scharle

Contents

Chapter 1 | Survey of Filing Systems and Career Skills   1

Chapter 2 | Card-Filing Names of Individuals   9

Chapter 3 | Card-Filing Business and Organization Names   27

Chapter 4 | Organizing Alphabetic Correspondence Files   45

Chapter 5 | Alphabetic Correspondence Filing Procedures   55

Chapter 6 | Subject Correspondence Filing Procedures   71

Chapter 7 | Organizing Your Work Station   87

Chapter 8 | Numeric Filing Systems   103

Chapter 9 | Geographic Filing Systems   113

Chapter 10 | Filing Systems for Modern Office Technology   121

Glossary   129

Index   134

Chapter

Survey of
Filing Systems
and
Career Skills

Competencies

1.1 Define *filing*.

1.2 State the purpose of filing in business.

1.3 Name jobs in which filing skills are needed.

1.4 Describe how filing may be used for job advancement.

1.5 Identify the skills needed in filing.

1.6 Identify the filing system that would be most useful for a given type of business.

1.7 Define *micrographics* and give two or more examples of the use of micrographics in business.

1.8 State the importance of the Freedom of Information Act and the Privacy Act to the file worker.

Purpose of a Filing System

1.1   Written communications—reports, letters, memorandums, order forms, and so on—are needed for the everyday operations of business firms and other organizations. If businesses are to stay in business and to operate efficiently, it is important for them to store these written communications in a standard, systematic manner. *Filing is simply the classifying, arranging, and storing of records so that they can be found quickly whenever they are needed.* So that anyone can file and find records easily and efficiently, a set of basic rules for filing must be followed by all.

1.2   Once you learn to use one ten-key adding machine, you can use any ten-key adding machine that has a similar keyboard. In the same way, once you know the basic rules of filing, you can file and find records rapidly as long as you follow the basic rules. Remember, files are of no value to a business if records cannot be found when they are needed. Thus we can say that the purpose of a filing system is *retrieval,* or the finding and removal of records from files.

Filing in Office Occupations

1.3   Filing will be one of your responsibilities when you accept an office job. Whether you work in a centralized filing department, or whether you keep files just for yourself, keep only some of your supervisor's files, or keep all of your supervisor's files, filing is a basic part of office work.

Filing as a Job Entry-Level Skill

If you can tell a person interviewing you that you know how to organize papers, file them in good order, and find them quickly, you will most likely make a favorable impression. Some office workers never bother to learn the basic rules for filing, yet the inability to locate a record when it is needed can throw an entire office into chaos. Every office occupation requires the knowledge of some kind of system for filing written records.

Secretaries, typists, stenographers, and other office workers all need filing skills to perform some of their job responsibilities, and more and more jobs now require filing as the primary responsibility of the office worker. Many organizations have centralized filing departments; these departments are staffed with skilled file workers. It is the responsibility of the file worker to classify and file records as well as to remove records from the files as they are requested by other departments. It is the job of some of these file workers to make sure that the records are returned to the filing department by a specific date.

The number of occupations that require filing skills has increased in the last decade. Computers, micrographics (the process of reducing records to miniature size), and word processing centers (offices or de-

Sybil Shelton/Monkmeyer

An interviewer will want to know if an applicant for an office position is able to take charge of files related to the job.

partments with automatic typewriters and other automatic equipment) have added to the number of jobs available for people with a knowledge of the fundamentals of filing.

Automatic data processing equipment has improved the efficiency of many businesses—large and small alike. However, the large volume of data that such machines produce has made it increasingly difficult to organize and file records. Not only is the *volume* of data that such automatic printers produce greater because of the speed of production, but the *size* of the paper on which computers print out records is usually larger than the standard sizes of paper used in offices. The media (or form) used as input for computers—punched cards, magnetic tape, or punched tape—must also be stored. Data processing employees require special skills for filing and finding such records.

Word processing centers have similar problems. The unusual media used by the machines, and the written records produced by such

A good way for a new employee to start learning the job is to consult the files.

machines, must be organized and filed in such a way that they can be found quickly when needed. As a word processing employee, part of your job may include the filing of documents and other kinds of records for use by you or others at a later date.

Filing in Management Positions

1.4 Knowing how to classify and how and where to store records is important for people who want to move into positions in records management and information processing. A records manager plans and sets up systems for organizing and controlling records. Information processing is another area where management positions are opening up. The manager of an information processing unit plans, sets up, and implements procedures for recording and distributing information within the company.

Filing in Other Occupations

1.3 Apart from its obvious importance in business, filing is a very useful skill in many other occupations. Doctors, lawyers, journalists, teachers, auto mechanics, cosmetologists, printers, electricians, and salespeople all use files at some point or other. It is worth your while to study hard and to learn that filing is not the mere putting away of records and forgetting about them! Filing is essential to business: without the *organization, protection,* and *control* of records, businesses cannot function.

Filing Skills, Attitudes, and Aptitudes

1.5 Skills in filing come with the knowledge of some very basic indexing rules. If each employee made up his or her own rules for filing information, no one else would be able to find that information. And even the person who made up the rules may soon forget them! So that anyone can file records and find them when they are needed, there must be a set of basic filing rules. For this reason, file workers must be skilled in the use of the alphabet and numbers, and they must know how to read and write numbers accurately. File workers should also be able to pay special attention to details. Some skill in handling papers and file folders is necessary; this can be further developed with experience. An attitude of promptness and efficiency is very important in order to assure that all records and communications are filed regularly. All in all, the file worker must be a good organizer.

The Four Basic Filing Systems

1.6 Records are filed in such a way that will make them easiest to find. There are four basic systems of filing: *alphabetic, subject, numeric,* and *geographic.* The alphabet in its proper order is used in all systems of filing because names usually provide the *captions* (the names or letters under which records are filed) for the storing of records.

In *alphabetic* systems, the captions are generally names of people or organizations. In *subject* systems, the captions are names of objects (usually products) or categories of information (such as advertising, travel expenses, personnel policies, and so on). In *numeric* systems, the captions are numbers that have been assigned to names and subjects. In *geographic* systems, the captions are names of places. Businesses and other kinds of organizations do not usually make use of all four systems. Instead, they use only those systems that best fit their needs. For example, organizations that handle a great deal of correspondence from other organizations or from individuals often find the alphabetic system of filing most useful. Using the letters of the alphabet in their proper order makes it possible to store correspondence according to the names of these organizations or individuals.

A business that deals with products, such as an office machines retail store, may wish to organize its files according to subject. Hence its files might have captions such as these: *Adding Machines, Bookkeeping Machines, Calculators, Dictation Equipment,* and so on.

Businesses such as drugstores that deal with prescription numbers, insurance companies that deal with policy numbers, government offices that issue licenses, and other businesses whose transactions are

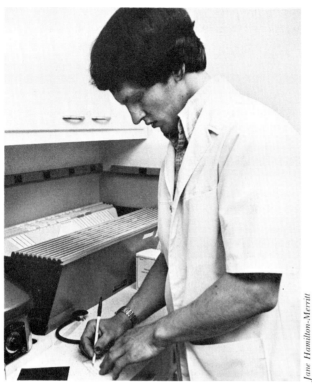

The ability to organize papers, file them, and *find them* is needed in almost every occupation.

identified by numbers, use a numeric filing system. Government offices that handle transactions with states or cities or other political divisions find it more efficient to file their records geographically. Businesses with branch offices, where sales are accounted for by territory, often use geographic files.

Sometimes one system will overlap another. For example, in an alphabetic system there may be a few cases where records can be filed more efficiently by subject. Correspondence might be filed according to the name of the correspondent, but records relating to employee vacations, for example, might be filed under *Employee Vacations.* In some subject systems, the name of a person or geographic title may appear. You will find that many of the statements made about the procedures and materials of, say, alphabetic filing apply to all other filing systems.

You will study each of these systems—alphabetic, subject, numeric, and geographic—in detail as you complete this text (and the *Progressive Filing Practice Set,* if you have it). The important thing to remember is that the basic goal of any filing system is retrieval. For this reason, businesses use those systems that are most efficient for their needs. Some businesses may need to use all four systems while others may use only one or two of them. Whatever the business, the system of filing used must be the one that is most convenient for people who work with—and are responsible for—files.

Micrographics

1.7   Besides the storing of business records in their original size, another well-established means of storing records is *micrographics,* or microphotography. This technique makes it possible for businesses to store records in reduced size. These records are maintained on microfilm and can be stored in single-frame lengths, on reels, or on sheets of film. The single-frame lengths are mounted on special cards that are called *aperture cards.* All these reduced records are called *microforms.* Once a record has been filmed, it can be viewed on a projector that enlarges it to its approximate original size. Since space can be a problem in maintaining records, the use of micrographics saves a considerable amount of money in storage space. For example, a single microfilm cabinet can hold, on rolls of film, the contents of at least 160 four-drawer file cabinets equipped to store letter-size records.

More and more often, banks are using microfilm to store copies of canceled checks. Department stores, dairies, and bus companies make use of microfilm in their billing operations. With the proper equipment, businesses can convert microfilm copy to original-size paper documents.

The Freedom of Information Act and the Privacy Act

1.8   In 1974 Congress passed two laws to protect the individual against misuse of information on file. One of these laws is the Freedom of Information Act, which gives you the right to ask for information that pertains to you. Examples of records which might be requested include those kept by doctors, dentists, lawyers, priests, and psychiatrists. Also, records of educational institutions, government agencies, and lending institutions that have information about you are available to read when you obtain permission from the organization that maintains those records.

The other law which was passed at the same time was called the Privacy Act. This law controls information which is readily available to the public. It serves to safeguard individual privacy. For someone to see your records within a particular organization, your permission is necessary.

What does this mean to you if you are a file worker? If you are responsible for files that are covered by the acts, you may have to screen people who request access to the files. You may be in charge of checking permission granted to people to use the files or to see that persons requesting various files sign a logbook. You also might have the authority to refuse access to certain records and documents. These responsibilities may make it necessary for you to qualify for a security classification in order to work for a government agency.

Hence we can say that the Freedom of Information Act allows you to see records about yourself. The Privacy Act limits those people who are allowed to see information about you in the files.

◆ HAVE YOU MET YOUR COMPETENCIES?

1.1 Define *filing*.

1.2 State the purpose of a filing system.

1.3 Name six jobs in which filing skills are needed.

1.4 Describe the possibilities for advancement in filing jobs.

1.5 Identify the skills needed in filing records.

1.6 Which system of filing would be used in each of the following examples?

Note: The last three examples may need more than one type of filing system.

1. Prescriptions in a drugstore.
2. Accounts in a billing department of a large department store.
3. Correspondence from a large number of people and organizations.
4. Records needed by a member of Congress who deals with a number of regions of the country.
5. A chemical company that deals with a variety of chemicals for industrial use.
6. A large food distribution company that has branch offices in thirty states.
7. A real estate firm that deals with twenty-one types of real estate.
8. An industrial kitchen equipment company that deals with people, organizations, and products.
9. An architect whose projects are identified by numbers and who has a large amount of correspondence in addition to those projects.
10. A merchandising firm whose accounts are listed by number but which also deals with products.

1.7 Define *micrographics* and give two or more examples of the use of micrographics in business.

1.8 State the importance of the Freedom of Information Act and the Privacy Act to the file worker.

Chapter

2

Card-Filing
Names of
Individuals

Competencies

2.1 Write or type the names of individuals in indexing order on file cards.

2.2 Alphabetize, using rough and fine sorting, and find cards on which names of individuals have been typed or written in indexing order.

2.3 Prepare alphabetic cross-reference cards containing names of individuals and arrange them in sequence with alphabetic cards.

2.4 State the importance of address files in the business office.

2.5 Name two types of equipment that can be used for the storage of address files.

2.6 Demonstrate the procedure for placing information on address cards.

2.7 Using an alphabetic card file with guides, file and find cards containing the names of individuals. Use appropriate rough and fine sorting procedures. (See Jobs 1 through 8 in the *Progressive Filing Practice Set.*)

2.8 Prepare alphabetic cross-reference cards and arrange them in sequence in an alphabetic card file. (See Jobs 6 and 7 in the *Progressive Filing Practice Set.*)

Just as there are rules for setting up a letter on the typewriter, there are also rules for filing records in the office. These rules are called *indexing rules*. Indexing rules determine the order in which records are filed. Such rules must be followed by everyone who uses files.

Fundamental Filing Terms

Before you learn the indexing rules, you must first become familiar with some of the filing terms that you will need to use.

2.2   **Alphabetic Arrangement.**   Indexing rules, you will see, are set up so that names are arranged according to the alphabet. Most people are already aware of this method, which is often called *alphabetizing*. For example, let us use the four names *Allen, Bryant, Morris,* and *Walters.* They are listed in that order because in the alphabet the first letter of *Allen* comes before the first letter of *Bryant.* The first letter of *Bryant* comes before the first letter of *Morris*, and the first letter of *Morris* comes before the first letter of *Walters.* The name *Burton* would follow *Bryant* because the second letter in *Burton* follows the second letter in *Bryant* in the alphabet even though the first letter of both names is the same.

Unit.   Each part of the name of a person or organization is called a *unit.* For example, in the name *Arthur Ray Allen* there are three units: *Arthur, Ray,* and *Allen.* Names of firms also have units, such as *Barretts Paper Container Company,* which has four units: *Barretts, Paper, Container,* and *Company.*

Indexing.   *Indexing* is the selection of a name or caption under which a record is to be filed. When you select a caption, you must determine the order in which the units are to be considered. For example, in the name *Margaret Ferguson,* indexing would occur when you were making the decision to file the record under the first name, *Margaret,* or under the last name, *Ferguson.* If you were deciding whether to file *Herman Ferguson* before or after *Margaret Ferguson,* you would also be indexing. The indexing process takes place *mentally,* and it is very important. Indexing must be completed before records are actually placed in the files.

Surname, Given Name, and Middle Name.   The name *Arthur Ray Allen* contains three parts: a surname, a given name, and a middle name. The last name, *Allen,* is the *surname;* the first name, *Arthur,* is the *given name;* and *Ray* is the *middle name.* You will use these terms again and again as you learn and apply the indexing rules.

The prevailing indexing rules are used in all businesses. The twenty-five rules presented in this chapter and in Chapter 3 are divided into five sections. The first two sections, in this chapter, deal with names of individuals. The last three sections, in Chapter 3, deal with names of firms and organizations, names of government agencies, and names of other institutions.

Following each section of rules, there are exercises in which you will use the rules you have learned. The exercises include practice on the rules you have just studied as well as on rules studied in previous sections.

RULE 1. ALPHABETIC ORDER

Alphabetize names by comparing the first units of the names letter by letter. Consider second units only when the first units are identical. Consider third units only when both the first and second are identical, and so on.

Note: If two names are identical, consider addresses (see Rule 18).

NAME	UNIT 1	UNIT 2	UNIT 3
Ajax	Ajax		
Baker	Baker		
Berkley	Berkley		
Berry Repairs	Berry	Repairs	
Berry Services	Berry	Services	
Carter Power Equipment	Carter	Power	Equipment
Carter Power Fixtures	Carter	Power	Fixtures

RULE 2. NOTHING COMES BEFORE SOMETHING

A name consisting of a single letter comes before a name consisting of a word that begins with the same letter. A name consisting of one word comes before a name that consists of the same word plus one or more other words. A name consisting of two or more words comes before a name that consists of the same two or more words plus another word, and so on.

NAME	UNIT 1	UNIT 2	UNIT 3
A	A		
Abbott Ballet	Abbott	Ballet	
Abbott Ballet Supplies	Abbott	Ballet	Supplies

RULE 3. LAST NAME FIRST

Treat each part of the name of an individual as a separate unit and consider the units in this order: surname (last name); given name (first name or initial); middle name or initial (if any).

NAME	UNIT 1	UNIT 2	UNIT 3
Lamb	Lamb		
C. Lamb	Lamb	C.	
C. George Lamb	Lamb	C.	George
Clara Lamb	Lamb	Clara	
Clara E. Lamb	Lamb	Clara	E.
A. Lambe	Lambe	A.	
Anna Lambe	Lambe	Anna	
Anna R. Lambe	Lambe	Anna	R.

Typing Names on File Cards

2.1
2.6

Typing names on file cards is a simple process. The six steps listed below should be used whenever such cards are typed.

1. Type the parts of the name in indexing order.

2. Begin typing the name four spaces from the left edge of the card on the second line from the top.

3. Some offices require that the entire name be capitalized. Most offices, however, prefer that the first letter of each important word be capitalized. Find out which style your company prefers and use that style consistently.

4. Some offices require that punctuation be omitted entirely, leaving two spaces where it would have been typed. Most offices, however, prefer normal punctuation. Again, whichever style your company prefers should be used consistently.

5. Use the style preferred by the company or the individual when typing file cards. For example, if a firm name is listed on the letterhead as *Baggett & Wilcox,* you should also use the *&* rather than *and.* Likewise, if *Express Moving and Storage Co.* spells out *and* but abbreviates *Company* on their letterhead, you should follow the same style.

6. To save time, some companies use the abbreviations *Co.* (for *Company*) and *Inc.* (for *Incorporated*) on their file cards and file labels.

Rough and Fine Sorting Techniques

2.2

Most file workers find it easier to work with the large number of papers (including cards) involved if they use rough and fine sorting processes.

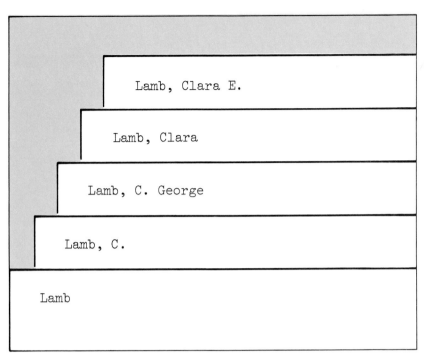

Names involving indexing rules 1, 2, and 3 as they should be typed on file cards.

This can be done with special sorting equipment or on a table or desk top. Follow these steps for sorting papers:

1. First, sort the papers into smaller stacks according to main divisions, such as letters of the alphabet. When you file a number of papers, you might first sort them by the letter of the alphabet under which the first indexing unit falls. For example, *Arthur, Arlen, Almond, Armagast, Albritten,* and *Aimes* would be in one stack while *Brigadoon, Babcock, Bobbett, Batiste,* and *Bond* would be in another, and so on. This is *rough sorting.*

2. Once the rough sorting is completed, the *fine sorting* takes place. The six "A" names would be further sorted alphabetically: *Aimes, Albritten, Almond, Arlen, Armagast,* and *Arthur.* Likewise, the "B" names would be sorted as follows: *Babcock, Batiste, Bobbett, Bond,* and *Brigadoon.*

   You will find that the filing exercises in this textbook will be easier—and will take much less time to complete—if you use rough and fine sorting techniques.

◆ FILING PRACTICE

The word *exercise* is used in the textbook; the word *job* is used in the *Progressive Filing Practice Set*. You may complete either the exercise or the job, or both, according to your teacher's instructions. Instructions for the jobs in the *Progressive Filing Practice Set* are given in the *Practice Instruction Manual* included in the set.

Complete Exercises 1 and 2 below and/or Job 1 in the *Progressive Filing Practice Set*.

Exercise 1

2.1 **A.** Write or type the following names in indexing order on 5 × 3 inch cards. The number beside each name should be written or typed in the upper right-hand corner of the card, as illustrated below.

1. Alberta P. Daswell
2. Arthur U. Hewitt
3. Andrew Mitler
4. James Henriksen
5. Douglas V. Miltenburg
6. Bron E. Milter
7. Beatrice Dasewell
8. Donald Hewit
9. Raymond Doswell
10. Lucas Miller

A name written in correct position on an unruled card.

Mitler, Andrew   3

Mitler, Andrew   3

A name typed in correct position on a ruled card.

2.2 **B.** Using rough and fine sorting techniques wherever necessary, alphabetize the ten cards above.

C. On a separate sheet of paper, similar to the one shown on page 15, list the numbers on the cards in the order in which they have been arranged. Turn in your answer sheet to your teacher for checking.

D. Save these ten cards for later use.

```
┌─────────────────────────────────────────────────────┐
│  Name  Your name        Exercise No. 1-C            │
│                                                       │
│   1.  7                   6.                          │
│                                                       │
│   2.  1                   7.                          │
│                                                       │
│   3.                      8.                          │
│                                                       │
│   4.                      9.                          │
│                                                       │
│   5.                     10.                          │
└─────────────────────────────────────────────────────┘
```

A partially completed answer sheet.

Exercise 2

2.1 **A.** Write or type the following names in indexing order on 5 × 3 inch cards. The number beside each name should be written or typed in the upper right-hand corner of the card.

11. Yvonne Slayden	**16.** M. L. Whiddon
12. J. Widdons	**17.** Maria R. Weaver
13. Clarence Whitten	**18.** Mildred Hart
14. D. Milboune West	**19.** Willie Slayton
15. Douglas Harcum	**20.** Cedrick Harte

2.2 **B.** Using rough and fine sorting techniques wherever necessary, alphabetize the ten cards above.

C. On a separate sheet of paper, similar to the one shown above, list the numbers on the cards in the order in which they have been arranged. Turn in your answer sheet to your teacher for checking.

D. Save these ten cards for later use.

RULE 4. PREFIXES

Consider a prefix (such as *Mc* in *McDonald*) as part of the name, not as a separate unit. Ignore variations in spacing, punctuation, or capitalization in names that contain prefixes (for example, *d'*, *D'*, *Da, de, De, Del, Des, Di, Du, Fitz, La, Le, M', Mac, O', St., Van, Van de, Van der, Von*, and *Von der*).

Note: Consider the prefixes *M'*, *Mac*, and *Mc* exactly as they are spelled.

Note: Alphabetize the prefix *St.* as though it were spelled *Saint*.

NAME	UNIT 1	UNIT 2	UNIT 3
Angel C. Dajon	Dajon	Angel	C.
Daniel J. D'Alesio	D'Alesio	Daniel	J.
Jason S. Macauley	Macauley	Jason	S.
Blanche MacCartney	MacCartney	Blanche	
McKenzie R. Matthews	Matthews	McKenzie	R.
Adele Frances McHenry	McHenry	Adele	Frances
Kay St. Pierre	Saint Pierre	Kay	
Gretchen A. Van der Berg	Van der Berg	Gretchen	A.
Walter Van de Riet	Van de Riet	Walter	

◆ FILING PRACTICE

2.7   Refer to the *Progressive Filing Practice Set,* if you are using it, for instructions to complete Job 2, which covers indexing rules 1, 2, 3, and 4. Otherwise, continue to Rule 5.

RULE 5. HYPHENATED INDIVIDUAL NAMES

Consider a hyphenated part of an individual's name as *one* indexing unit. Ignore the hyphen.

NAME	UNIT 1	UNIT 2	UNIT 3
Pauline R. Munden-Brown	Munden-Brown	Pauline	R.
George-Anne Munsey	Munsey	George-Anne	
Joyce M. Munson	Munson	Joyce	M.
Joyce-Marie Munson	Munson	Joyce-Marie	
Sherman T. Murrell-Moore	Murrell-Moore	Sherman	T.

◆ FILING PRACTICE

2.7   Complete Job 3 in the *Progressive Filing Practice Set,* if you are using it. Otherwise, continue to Rule 6.

RULE 6. TITLES

Ignore a title used with the last name plus one or more other parts of an individual's name, but consider a title as the first unit if it is used with only one part of an individual's name.

Note: Consider the title *Mrs.* if a woman uses her husband's name and you do not know her first name. Treat *Mrs.* as it is spelled.

NAME	UNIT 1	UNIT 2	UNIT 3
Congressman Steven A. Boyd	Boyd	Steven	A.
Chief Childress	Chief	Childress	
Dr. Roger Davis	Davis	Roger	
Mrs. Roger Davis (whose own first name is not known)	Davis	Roger	Mrs.
Mrs. Neil Ellis (whose own first name is known to be Geraldine)	Ellis	Geraldine	
Mr. Neil Ellis	Ellis	Neil	

RULE 7. SENIORITY TERMS AND OTHER DESIGNATIONS FOLLOWING THE NAME

Ignore a seniority term (such as *Sr., Jr., II,* and *III*), a professional degree (such as *CPA, M.D.,* and *Ph.D.*), and any other designation following a name.

NAME	UNIT 1	UNIT 2	UNIT 3
Catherine A. O'Connor, CAPT	O'Connor	Catherine	A.
Thomas J. O'Connor, II	O'Connor	Thomas	J.
Merle Painter, M.D.	Painter	Merle	
Jason M. Palmer*	Palmer	Jason	M.
Jason M. Palmer, Jr.*	Palmer	Jason	M.

*__Note:__ For indexing purposes, these two names are considered identical and are therefore arranged according to address (see Rule 18).

◆ FILING PRACTICE

2.7   Complete Job 4 in the *Progressive Filing Practice Set,* if you are using it. Otherwise, continue to Rule 8.

RULE 8. ABBREVIATED NAMES AND NICKNAMES

Consider any abbreviated part of a name (such as *Wm.* for *William* or *Robt.* for *Robert*) as though it were written in full.

Consider a name such as *Al* for *Alfred* or *Kate* for *Katherine* only if it is the true name rather than a nickname or if the true name is not known.

NAME	UNIT 1	UNIT 2	UNIT 3
Geo. N. Riggs	Riggs	George	N.
William (Billy) Riley	Riley	William	
Billy C. Riner	Riner	Billy	C.
Judith (Judy) M. Ritchey	Ritchey	Judith	M.
Jas. L. Rivenbark	Rivenbark	James	L.

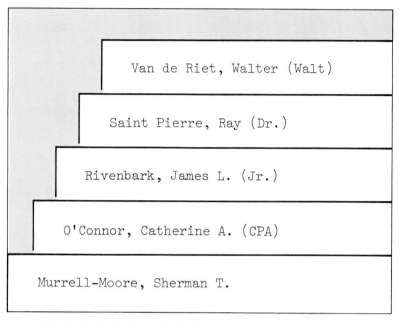

Van de Riet, Walter (Walt)

Saint Pierre, Ray (Dr.)

Rivenbark, James L. (Jr.)

O'Connor, Catherine A. (CPA)

Murrell-Moore, Sherman T.

Names involving indexing rules 4 through 8 as they should be typed on file cards.

◆ FILING PRACTICE

2.7 Complete Exercises 3 through 5 below and/or Job 5 in the *Progressive Filing Practice Set,* if you are using it.

Exercise 3

2.1 **A.** Write or type the following names in indexing order on 5 × 3 inch cards. The number beside each name should be written or typed in the upper right-hand corner of the card.

21. M. Santo D'Asaro
22. Wm. A. Sampson-Brown
23. Isabel Martin
24. Rolfe Da Mato
25. Marie-Caroline Sanipy
26. Fredericka Maas, CPA
27. Irving MacDuff, Jr.
28. Vincent Leonne Dai-Ichi
29. Lin Ma-Hial-Tsuing
30. Anthony P. D'Agostino

2.2 **B.** Using rough and fine sorting techniques wherever necessary, alphabetize the ten cards above.

C. On a separate sheet of paper, similar to the one shown on page 15, list the numbers on the cards in the order in which they have been arranged. Turn in your answer sheet to your teacher for checking.

D. Save these ten cards for later use.

Exercise 4

2.1 **A.** Write or type the following names in indexing order on 5x3 inch cards. The number beside each name should be written or typed in the upper right-hand corner of the card.

31. Jas. W. MacDulley   **36.** Robt. Hartley
32. Yoo Souy   **37.** Gilbert P. Mott, II
33. Sally Hall-Martindale **38.** Henry David Westover
34. D. R. McArthur, Ph.D. **39.** N. Abraham Harken
35. Jowanda St. Germaine   **40.** David A. Weilgus, Jr.

2.2 **B.** Using rough and fine sorting techniques wherever necessary, alphabetize the ten cards above.

C. On a separate sheet of paper, list the numbers on the cards in the order in which they have been arranged. Turn in your answer sheet to your teacher for checking.

D. Save these ten cards for later use.

Exercise 5

2.1 **A.** Write or type the following names in indexing order on 5 x 3 inch cards. The number beside each name should be written or typed in the upper right-hand corner of the card.

41. Harold Danielson   **46.** Regina Michele
42. A. James Mitler   **47.** D. Elizabeth St. Thomas
43. Stuart Michael   **48.** Harold Samuel
44. Harris William   **49.** Claudette A. DuPree
45. Marie-Elena Danielsen **50.** Harold Sampson

2.2 **B.** Using rough and fine sorting techniques wherever necessary, alphabetize the ten cards above.

C. On a separate sheet of paper, list the numbers on the cards in the order in which they have been arranged. Turn in your answer sheet to your teacher for checking.

D. Save these ten cards for later use.

Cross-Referencing With Cards

2.3   It is sometimes difficult to know what part of an individual's name is the surname and what part is the given name. Should such a situation ever arise, simply list the name as it normally appears and cross-reference it in the files under the name as it would appear when transposed.

Filed Under	Cross-Reference
Brandon, Barrett	Barrett, Brandon
Donald, Joseph	Joseph, Donald
William, Fletcher	Fletcher, William

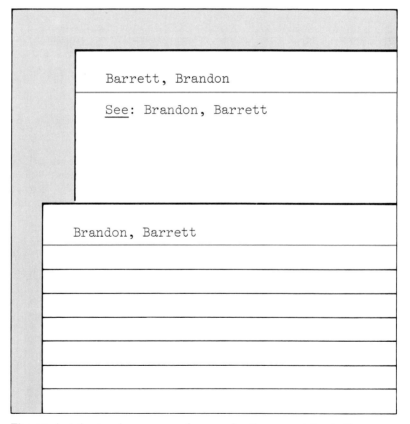

The card at the top is a cross-reference for the one at the bottom.

◆ FILING PRACTICE

2.7   Complete Exercises 6 and 7 below and/or Jobs 6 through 8 in the
2.8   *Progressive Filing Practice Set,* if you are using it.

Exercise 6

A. Arrange cards 1 through 50 in numeric order (**Example:** 1, 2, 3, 4, and so on).

2.2 **B.** Alphabetize those fifty cards using rough and fine sorting techniques wherever necessary. At the same time, cross-reference the following names:

1. Lin Ma-Hial-Tsuing, Card 29; cross-reference under *Ma-Hial-Tsuing Lin,* card 29x.
2. Stuart Michael, card 43; cross-reference under *Michael Stuart,* card 43x.
3. Harris William, card 44; cross-reference under *William Harris,* card 44x.
4. Harold Samuel, card 48; cross-reference under *Samuel Harold,* card 48x.

Note: The cross-reference cards will, of course, be placed where the first unit of the name on the card occurs in the alphabet.

C. On a separate sheet of paper, list the numbers on the cards in the order in which they have been arranged, including the cross-reference cards where they occur. Turn in your answer sheet to your teacher for checking.

D. Leave the fifty cards and four cross-reference cards as you arranged them for use in Exercise 7.

Exercise 7

2.2 **A.** Using the fifty cards that were alphabetized in Exercise 6, find the cards listed below as fast as possible. The real proof of filing expertise is in the finding. Speed is essential, because a worker's time can be wasted if a record cannot be located promptly.

Raymond Doswell	Douglas V. Miltenburg
Yvonne Slayden	Cedrick Harte
Clarence Whitten	Douglas Harcum
Robt. Hartley	Yoo Souy
Marie-Elena Danielsen	D. Elizabeth St. Thomas

B. On a sheet of paper, write the names and card numbers in four columns similar to the way it has been done in the illustration on page 22. Hand in this answer sheet for checking.

C. Save cards 1 through 50 and the four cross-reference cards for use at the end of Chapter 3.

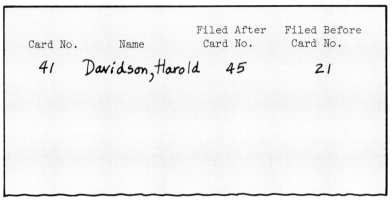

Card No.	Name	Filed After Card No.	Filed Before Card No.
41	Davidson, Harold	45	21

A partially completed answer sheet for Exercise 7.

Card Files

In many offices, a great deal of important information—such as names, addresses, and telephone numbers—is kept in *card files.* Card files are used to organize information that would otherwise be listed on sheets of paper in a bound or loose-leaf book. Storing records in card files makes it easy to locate information, to add new information or remove old information, and to rearrange information in any sequence.

2.4   Possibly the most often used card files are *address files.* An address file—as well as any other kind of card file—might be kept in a box on the desk or on a rotary wheel file such as the one illustrated on page 23. By using such files an office worker can locate a customer's address and telephone number quickly and efficiently. Businesses, no matter how large or how small, use address files for reference as well as for mailing lists.

Card files may be used to record new information on a continuous basis. For example, in a doctor's office changes or additions are made on a ledger card each time a patient comes to the office. The account is updated as necessary. These files are called *posted card records.* Card files may also be used to provide reference to existing information; these are called *index card records.* An address card file would be an index card record.

There are many types of cards available as well as cards specially designed to fit equipment that has been custom-made for a particular job. When deciding what type of card to purchase, these six questions should be asked:

1. Will this card be used permanently or temporarily?
2. How often will this card be handled?
3. Will the card be used for reference purposes only, or is it to be used to record information? If the card is to be used to record information, will that information be recorded by hand or by machine?

4. Is the card to be stored in a vertical or a visible card file? (In a *vertical card file,* cards are stored on edge; in a *visible card file,* equipment is specially designed so that the information on the edges of cards may be seen without handling the cards.)
5. Is a transparent covering used on the card for protection, or is the card unprotected?
6. Is it desirable to have specially colored cards for purposes of classification?

File cards are sold in various weights—light, medium, heavy, and extra heavy. They are available in various finishes, from smooth to rough. Some file cards are suitable for use in machine- or hand-posting. Some have special plastic covers that protect them from smudges and tearing. Some visible card files may have a protective plastic edge on the card where it is to be handled a great deal.

File cards come in various colors; this aids the office worker in classifying records. For example, if an address file is used for mailing lists, the mailing list for prospective customers could be recorded on green cards, while addresses of manufacturers could be recorded on blue cards. In this way, an office worker would not have to look through all the file cards to find the address of a particular manufacturer.

Whatever the job, and whatever the type of card to be purchased, it is important to remember that the price of the best cards may well be worth it. If the record is for short-term use, it is not necessary to buy high-quality cards. However, if a card will not last as long as a record is needed, the cost of retyping a new card will be much greater than the cost of the high-quality card that should have been used in the first place.

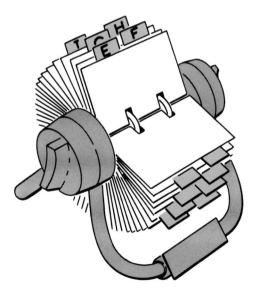

The rotary wheel index card file is kept on the worker's desk to provide immediate reference to important addresses.

Vertical Card Files

2.5 Vertical card files are frequently used for posted card records. For example, customer ledger cards in a bank are often kept in this kind of file. Vertical card files are also used for index records, such as address files. These records are organized in drawers or open cabinets with guides in much the same way as correspondence files are organized. In this case, however, there are no folders. Each card contains a separate name, address, subject, product name, or other information. Vertical card files are very compact—a great deal of information can be stored in a small place. This is a great advantage to businesses, since space costs money.

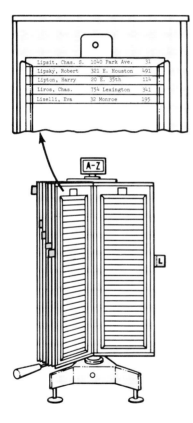

Vertical rotary racks for index card records of names and addresses.

Standard cards for vertical card files measure 5 by 3 inches, 6 by 4 inches, or 8 by 5 inches. The side the card rests on when it is stored is the first dimension given. Tabulated, or punched, cards that are used in data processing measure $7\frac{3}{8}$ by $3\frac{1}{4}$ inches. Punched-card files are kept in offices that use data processing machines.

The size of the card should be directly related to the amount and kind of information to be recorded on it. So that you can quickly and accurately find cards that have been filed, there should be at least one guide for every twenty-five to fifty cards.

Typing on Vertical-Record Cards

2.6　When you prepare cards for this kind of file, type the caption on the second line from the top of the card. Any additional key information should be kept as close to the caption as possible so that it may be read without removing the card from the file.

Visible Card Files

2.5　Visible card files, or visible files for short, are often used for index-card records, such as address files, although they can also be used for posted records. Cards for visible files are stored horizontally in drawers with the edges overlapping. They may also be stored on vertical rotary racks, in large tubs, on rotary wheels, or in loose-leaf visible books. No matter how the cards are stored, visible files make it possible to find vital information quickly. Visible files are often used by receptionists who need to locate information for waiting visitors.

Visible card files require no separate guides since each card, being partly visible, acts as its own guide. Visible files make *signaling* easier than in vertical files. In visible files, plastic, metal, or paper devices are used to guide the eye, and information can be indicated by the position, color, or both, of insert slips or signal tabs. Signaling of this type makes important facts stand out and ensures appropriate action. Take a look at the visible card file illustrated on page 26.

It would be more practical to use a rotary rack than a horizontal-drawer visible file for the location of telephone numbers by an information operator. Hence we can say that the specific needs of an organization in regard to volume, location, portability, and type of use should all be considered in determining what type of equipment to purchase. Traveling sales representatives often use a loose-leaf book of some sort that keeps important records handy as customers are visited. When information is to be handwritten on a card file, a horizontal-drawer visible file would provide a better writing surface than, say, a rotary wheel file. When the information is to be posted by machine, a tub file is more efficient than a rotary rack because the cards can be removed easily from the file.

Typing on Visible-Record Cards

2.6　When information is typed on cards to be filed in visible equipment, the caption should come as close to the visible edge as possible. Because most of these cards are stored so that they overlap, it is important to type the information so that it is not covered by the card that overlaps it.

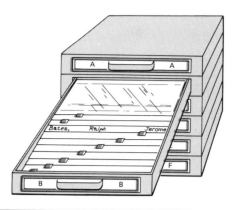

Bates,	Ralph	Jerome
LAST NAME	**FIRST NAME**	**INITIAL**
Parent or Guardian	William E. Bates	
Address	219 Grove Drive	
	Toledo, OH 43608	
Telephone No.	555-9112	
Date Entered	September 2, 19--	
Previous School	Fox Junior	
Assigned Class	10th	
Assigned Room	40	
Date Removed		
Reason Removed		
LAST NAME	**FIRST NAME**	**INITIAL**
Bates,	Ralph	Jerome

The card is inserted in the visible file so that the caption at the bottom is visible.

◆ HAVE YOU MET YOUR COMPETENCIES?

2.1
TO 2.3 Have you successfully completed Exercises 1 through 7 in this chapter?

2.4 State the importance of address files in the business office.

2.5 Name two types of equipment that can be used to store address files.

2.6 If supplies permit, using the names and addresses of ten of your classmates, demonstrate the procedure for placing information on address cards. If supplies do not permit, explain the steps in the procedure for placing information on address cards.

2.7 Have you successfully completed Jobs 1 through 8 in the *Progressive Fil-*
2.8 *ing Practice Set?*

Chapter

3

Card-Filing
Business and
Organization
Names

Competencies

3.1   Write or type business and organization names in indexing order on file cards.

3.2   Alphabetize and find cards on which business and organization names have been typed or written in indexing order.

3.3   State an example in which an indexing rule might be varied or changed to meet the needs of a special business situation.

3.4   Prepare alphabetic cross-reference cards containing business and organization names and arrange them in sequence with alphabetic cards.

3.5   Using an alphabetic card file with guides, file and find cards containing business and organization names. (See Jobs 9 through 24 in the *Progressive Filing Practice Set.*)

3.6   Prepare alphabetic cross-reference cards and arrange them in sequence in an alphabetic card file. (See Jobs 20 and 21 in the *Progressive Filing Practice Set.*)

Just as there are specific rules to follow when indexing and filing names of individuals, there are also specific rules that must be followed when indexing names of businesses and organizations. These rules are presented in this chapter in three sections. The first section contains seven rules which are basic to the filing of business and organization names. The second section involves three rules dealing with numbers in the name of a business firm as well as geographic parts of firm names and addresses. The third section deals with the last seven rules that apply to specific institutions and government names.

RULE 9. FIRST WORD FIRST

Treat each word in the name of a business firm as a separate unit and consider the units in the same order as they are written. **Exception:** When the name of a business firm includes the last name plus one or more other parts of an individual's name, transpose only the parts of the individual's name (last name first—see Rule 3).

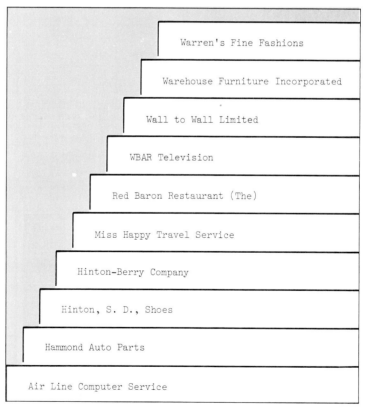

Warren's Fine Fashions

Warehouse Furniture Incorporated

Wall to Wall Limited

WBAR Television

Red Baron Restaurant (The)

Miss Happy Travel Service

Hinton-Berry Company

Hinton, S. D., Shoes

Hammond Auto Parts

Air Line Computer Service

Names involving indexing rules 9 through 15 as they should be typed on file cards.

NAME	UNIT 1	UNIT 2	UNIT 3	UNIT 4
Hammond Auto Parts	Hammond	Auto	Parts	
Harris Office Supplies	Harris	Office	Supplies	
Hilltop Music Center	Hilltop	Music	Center	
Hilton Decorators	Hilton	Decorators		
S. D. Hinton Shoes	Hinton	S.	D.	Shoes
Julian Hirst Hobby Shop	Hirst	Julian	Hobby	Shop
Esther Hobbs Needlework Center	Hobbs	Esther	Needlework	Center
James Hodges Drug Company	Hodges	James	Drug	Company

Note: Consider a title in a firm name as an indexing unit. Treat abbreviated titles as if they were written in full, except *Mr., Mrs.,* and *Ms.*

NAME	UNIT 1	UNIT 2	UNIT 3	UNIT 4
Docktor Pet Center	Docktor	Pet	Center	
Dr. Dennon Clothes	Doctor	Dennon	Clothes	
Miss Happy Travel Service	Miss	Happy	Travel	Service
Mister Tastee	Mister	Tastee		
Mr. Tux Rentals	Mr.	Tux	Rentals	
Mrs. Simms Foods	Mrs.	Simms	Foods	

RULE 10. ARTICLES, CONJUNCTIONS, AND PREPOSITIONS

Ignore an article, conjunction, or preposition (such as *a, an, and, for, in, of,* or *the*) in the name of a business firm unless it is a distinctive part of the name.

NAME	UNIT 1	UNIT 2	UNIT 3	UNIT 4
Academy of Hair Design	Academy	Hair	Design	
The Barn on the Beach	Barn	Beach		
Cap and Quill Restaurant	Cap	Quill	Restaurant	
Packed in a Box Chicken	Packed	Box	Chicken	
Time of Your Life Amusements	Time	Your	Life	Amusements
Wall to Wall, Limited	Wall	Wall	Limited	

In the following examples, the prepositions *For, Out, Over,* and *Under* are considered to be distinctive parts of the names and are therefore indexing units.

NAME	UNIT 1	UNIT 2	UNIT 3	UNIT 4
For Music Lovers, Incorporated	For	Music	Lovers	Incorporated
Out West Dude Ranch	Out	West	Dude	Ranch
Over You Umbrellas	Over	You	Umbrellas	
Under the Oaks Restaurant	Under	Oaks	Restaurant	

◆ FILING PRACTICE

3.5 Complete Job 9 in the *Progressive Filing Practice Set,* if you are using it. Otherwise, continue to Rule 11.

RULE 11. ABBREVIATIONS

Treat an abbreviated word in a firm name as though the word were written in full.

NAME	UNIT 1	UNIT 2	UNIT 3	UNIT 4
Barclay Mfg. Co.	Barclay	Manufacturing	Company	
International Sterling, Ltd.	International	Sterling	Limited	
Soroko Bros. Market	Soroko	Brothers	Market	
Trim Rite Beef Co.	Trim	Rite	Beef	Company
Warehouse Furniture Inc.	Warehouse	Furniture	Incorporated	

RULE 12. SINGLE LETTERS

Consider single letters that are not abbreviations as separate units, whether they are separated by spaces or not.

Note: Single letters that are hyphenated should be considered as one unit (see Rule 13).

NAME	UNIT 1	UNIT 2	UNIT 3	UNIT 4	UNIT 5
AAA Rental Mart	A	A	A	Rental	Mart
C R Electric Co.	C	R	Electric	Company	
WWVA Radio	W	W	V	A	Radio

◆ FILING PRACTICE

3.5 Complete Job 10 in the *Progressive Filing Practice Set,* if you are using it. Otherwise, continue to Rule 13.

RULE 13. HYPHENATED FIRM NAMES

Consider hyphenated parts of a firm name as one unit.

NAME	UNIT 1	UNIT 2	UNIT 3
Anderson Lock-Smith Co.	Anderson	Lock-Smith	Company
Anderson-Little Printing Co.	Anderson-Little	Printing	Company
The Car Wash Center	Car	Wash	Center
Car-Truck Leasing Co.	Car-Truck	Leasing	Company

RULE 14. ONE OR TWO WORDS

Consider as one unit a part of a firm name that may be written as one word, as two words, or with a hyphen.

NAME	UNIT 1	UNIT 2	UNIT 3
Alta Air Lines, Inc.	Alta	Air Lines	Incorporated
Candlelight Diner	Candlelight	Diner	
Candle-Light Gift Shop	Candle-Light	Gift	Shop
Candle Light Manor	Candle Light	Manor	
Northwest Investors, Inc.	Northwest	Investors	Incorporated
North West Villa	North West	Villa	

◆ FILING PRACTICE

3.5   Complete Job 11 in the *Progressive Filing Practice Set,* if you are using it. Otherwise, continue to Rule 15.

RULE 15. POSSESSIVES AND CONTRACTIONS

Ignore the apostrophe and consider all letters in a possessive or a contraction.

NAME	UNIT 1	UNIT 2	UNIT 3	UNIT 4
Bond's Service Station	Bond's	Service	Station	
Linda E. Clements	Clements	Linda	E.	
Ross Clement's Insurance Co.	Clement's	Ross	Insurance	Company
That's Fine Fashions	That's	Fine	Fashions	

◆ FILING PRACTICE

3.5   Complete Exercises 1 and 2 below.

Exercise 1

3.1   **A.** Write or type the following names in indexing order on 5 × 3 inch cards. The number beside each name should be written or typed in the upper right-hand corner of the card.

51. Lucien B. Miller
52. Walter Samul
53. Dial a Steak
54. Down Town Seafood Shop
55. Jos. L. Wilmotte & Co., Inc.
56. Meena-Arjan Imports-Exports, Ltd.
57. W K International Inks

58. Deli-O Sandwich Shop
59. Downtown Restaurant
60. Whitten & Minnetree Electronics Co.

3.2   **B.** Using rough and fine sorting techniques wherever necessary, alphabetize the ten cards above.

C. On a separate sheet of paper, list the numbers on the cards in the order in which they have been arranged. Turn in your answer sheet to your teacher for checking.

D. Save these ten cards for later use.

Exercise 2

3.1   **A.** Write or type the following names in indexing order on 5 × 3 inch cards. The number beside each name should be written or typed in the upper right-hand corner of the card.

61. D B A Steakhouse
62. Sampson & Hewitt Mfg. Co.
63. Weaver Marina
64. Hy-Gus Cafe
65. Slayden Zebra Farm
66. McArthur & Whiten Insurance Co., Inc.
67. Holly-Day Plants
68. Ed Whitteaker Lumber Co.
69. Hall-Maine Food Brokers, Inc.
70. Dee Dee Service Station

3.2   **B.** Using rough and fine sorting techniques wherever necessary, alphabetize the ten cards above.

C. On a separate sheet of paper, list the numbers on the cards in the order in which they have been arranged. Turn in your answer sheet to your teacher for checking.

D. Save these ten cards for later use.

RULE 16. NUMBERS

Consider a number in the name of a business firm as though it were written in words, and treat it as one unit. Express the number in as few

NAME	UNIT 1	UNIT 2	UNIT 3	UNIT 4
Conley's 88 Products	Conley's	Eighty-Eight	Products	
5th Street Restaurant	Fifth	Street	Restaurant	
4 Phase Systems, Inc.	Four	Phase	Systems	Incorporated
1440 Duke Street Apartments	Fourteen Hundred Forty	Duke	Street	Apartments
Two-Twenty Cosmetics, Ltd.	Two-Twenty	Cosmetics	Limited	

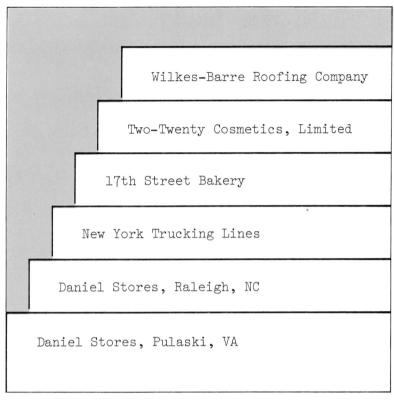

Wilkes-Barre Roofing Company

Two-Twenty Cosmetics, Limited

17th Street Bakery

New York Trucking Lines

Daniel Stores, Raleigh, NC

Daniel Stores, Pulaski, VA

Names involving indexing rules 16 through 18 as they should be typed on file cards.

words as possible. For example, treat *1,420* as *fourteen hundred twenty,* not *one thousand four hundred twenty.*

◆ FILING PRACTICE

3.5 Complete Job 12 in the *Progressive Filing Practice Set,* if you are using it. Otherwise, continue to Rule 17.

RULE 17. PARTS OF GEOGRAPHIC NAMES

Consider each part of a geographic name as a separate indexing unit.
Exception: Treat hyphenated parts of a geographic name as one unit.

NAME	UNIT 1	UNIT 2	UNIT 3	UNIT 4
Ann Arbor Bottling Co.	Ann	Arbor	Bottling	Company
Costa Rica Cereals	Costa	Rica	Cereals	
Des Moines Plumbing & Heating	Des	Moines	Plumbing	Heating
Eau Claire Dairy Works	Eau	Claire	Dairy	Works
El Salvador Oil Co.	El	Salvador	Oil	Company
Ft. Lauderdale Builders Association	Fort	Lauderdale	Builders	Association
Wilkes-Barre Roofing Co.	Wilkes-Barre	Roofing	Company	

RULE 18. ADDRESSES

When two names are identical, alphabetize by comparing parts of addresses in the following order.

First: city or town

Second: state (Consider the state only if the city or town names are the same; for example, *Charleston, South Carolina,* and *Charleston, West Virginia.*)

Third: street name (If the street name is a number, treat it as if it were spelled out.)

Fourth: direction (For example, *north, south, northwest, southwest.*)

Fifth: house or building number (Arrange in numeric order from lowest to highest.)

NAME	UNIT 1	UNIT 2	UNIT 3	UNIT 4	UNIT 5
Shoney's Athens, Georgia	Shoney's	Athens			
Shoney's Bridgeport, Connecticut	Shoney's	Bridgeport	Connecticut		
Shoney's Bridgeport, Ohio	Shoney's	Bridgeport	Ohio		
Shoney's 14th Street Denver, Colorado	Shoney's	Denver	Fourteenth	Street	
Shoney's Hilltop Avenue, Northeast Denver, Colorado	Shoney's	Denver	Hilltop	Avenue	Northeast
Shoney's Hilltop Avenue, Southwest Denver, Colorado	Shoney's	Denver	Hilltop	Avenue	Southwest
Shoney's 147 Military Highway Denver, Colorado	Shoney's	Denver	Military	Highway	147
Shoney's 490 Military Highway Denver, Colorado	Shoney's	Denver	Military	Highway	490

◆ FILING PRACTICE

3.5 Complete Exercises 3 and 4 below and/or Jobs 13 through 16 in the *Progressive Filing Practice Set,* if you are using it.

Exercise 3

3.1 **A.** Write or type the following names in indexing order on 5 × 3 inch cards. The number beside each name should be written or typed in the upper right-hand corner of the card.

71. 7th Avenue Disco

72. Weaver's Furs
  1819 41st Street

73. 76 Trombones & Instruments, Co.
74. Winston-Salem Recreation Center
75. Weaver's Furs
    2208 Fifth Avenue
76. Sam's 45's Record Shop
77. Walla Walla Salt Water Fishermen's Association
78. Hundred Best Books
79. 77 Foods, Inc.
80. Weaver's Furs
    901 41st Street

3.2 **B.** Using rough and fine sorting techniques wherever necessary, alphabetize the ten cards above.

C. On a separate sheet of paper, list the numbers on the cards in the order in which they have been arranged. Turn in your answer sheet to your teacher for checking.

D. Save these ten cards for later use.

Exercise 4

3.1 **A.** Write or type the following names in indexing order on 5 × 3 inch cards. The number beside each name should be written or typed in the upper right-hand corner of the card.

81. Million-Seller Records
82. Sixth Street Pharmacy
83. Hewitt Automotive Supply, Portland, Oregon
84. Montague's Desks & Office Equipment
85. Montclair Manufacturers
86. St. Petersburg Brewery
87. Mt. Rainier Ski Slopes
88. Hot Springs Lodge
89. Minneapolis and St. Paul Coliseum
90. Hewitt Automotive Supply, Portland, Maine

3.2 **B.** Using rough and fine sorting techniques wherever necessary, alphabetize the ten cards above.

C. On a separate sheet of paper, list the numbers on the cards in the order in which they have been arranged. Turn in your answer sheet to your teacher for checking.

D. Save these ten cards for later use.

RULE 19. BANKS AND OTHER FINANCIAL INSTITUTIONS

Consider each part of the name of a bank or other financial institution in the same order as it is written.

NAME	UNIT 1	UNIT 2	UNIT 3	UNIT 4
American National Bank	American	National	Bank	
Bank of the Commonwealth	Bank	Commonwealth		
Citizen's Trust Bank	Citizen's	Trust	Bank	
First Savings & Loan Co.	First	Savings	Loan	Company
Parkersburg National Bank	Parkersburg	National	Bank	

RULE 20. HOTELS AND MOTELS

Consider each part of the name of a hotel or a motel in the same order as it is written. If the word *Hotel* or *Motel* appears at the beginning of the name, consider the distinctive part of the name first.

NAME	UNIT 1	UNIT 2	UNIT 3
Atlantic Hotel	Atlantic	Hotel	
The Hotel Dunes	Dunes	Hotel	
Executive Park Motel	Executive	Park	Motel
The Motel Flagship	Flagship	Motel	

◆ FILING PRACTICE

3.5 Complete Job 17 in the *Progressive Filing Practice Set,* if you are using it. Otherwise, continue to Rule 21.

RULE 21. HOSPITALS AND RELIGIOUS INSTITUTIONS

Consider each part of the name of a hospital or a religious institution in the same order as it is written.

NAME	UNIT 1	UNIT 2	UNIT 3
Bayberry Psychiatric Hospital	Bayberry	Psychiatric	Hospital
Community Health Center	Community	Health	Center
Mission of God Church	Mission	God	Church

RULE 22. EDUCATIONAL INSTITUTIONS

Consider each part of the name of a university, college, high school, elementary school, or library, in the same order as it is written. If a word like *University* or *College* appears at the beginning of the name, consider the distinctive parts of the name first.

Note: Transpose names of individuals (see Rule 3).

NAME	UNIT 1	UNIT 2	UNIT 3	UNIT 4
University of Baltimore	Baltimore	University		
Belmont Public Library	Belmont	Public	Library	
Carroll High School	Carroll	High	School	
Central Michigan University	Central	Michigan	University	
Louise Luxford Elementary School	Luxford	Louise	Elementary	School
College of William and Mary	William	Mary	College	

◆ FILING PRACTICE

3.5 Complete Job 18 in the *Progressive Filing Practice Set,* if you are using it. Otherwise, continue to Rule 23.

RULE 23. FEDERAL GOVERNMENT NAMES

Index a name that pertains to the federal government under *United States Government* (first three units). Then consider the name of the department, and finally the name of the bureau, division, commission, board, or other subdivision. (**Remember:** In the following examples, the first three units are *United States Government.*)

NAME	UNIT 4	UNIT 5	UNIT 6	UNIT 7	UNIT 8
U.S. Agriculture Dept. Food Nutrition Service	Agriculture	Department	Food	Nutrition	Service
U.S. Agriculture Dept. Meat Inspection Division	Agriculture	Department	Meat	Inspection	Division
U.S. Commerce Dept. National Weather Service	Commerce	Department	National	Weather	Service
U.S. Department of Defense Investigative Services	Defense	Department	Investigative	Services	

RULE 24. STATE AND LOCAL GOVERNMENT NAMES

Index a name that pertains to a state, county, city, or town under the distinctive name, underlined followed by the word *state, county, city, town,* or other classification. Consider the classification as an indexing unit whether or not it appears in the name as written. Finally, consider the name of the department, bureau, division, board, or other subdivision.

NAME	UNIT 1	UNIT 2	UNIT 3	UNIT 4
Arizona Department of Education	Arizona	State	Education	Department
Department of Sanitation City of Fairmont	Fairmont	City	Sanitation	Department
Finance Department Marion County	Marion	County	Finance	Department
Division of Highways State of Missouri	Missouri	State	Highways	Division

RULE 25. FOREIGN GOVERNMENT NAMES

Consider a name that pertains to a foreign government first under the distinctive name of the country, followed by the classification *Dominion, Republic, Kingdom,* or other designation, then under the name of the governmental department or other subdivision.

NAME	UNIT 1	UNIT 2	UNIT 3	UNIT 4	UNIT 5
Republic of Central Africa Department of Agriculture	Central	Africa	Republic	Agriculture	Department

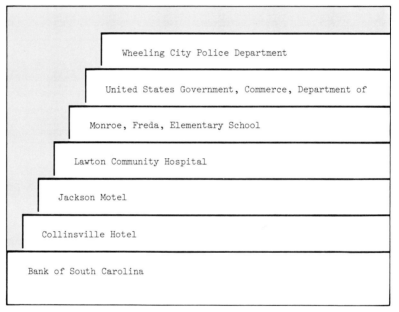

```
Wheeling City Police Department
United States Government, Commerce, Department of
Monroe, Freda, Elementary School
Lawton Community Hospital
Jackson Motel
Collinsville Hotel
Bank of South Carolina
```

Names involving indexing rules 19 through 25 as they should be typed on file cards.

◆ FILING PRACTICE

3.5 Complete Exercises 5 through 7 below and/or Job 19 in the *Progressive Filing Practice Set,* if you are using it.

Exercise 5
3.1 **A.** Write or type the following names in indexing order on 5 × 3 inch cards. The number beside each name should be written or typed in the upper right-hand corner of the card.

91. The State Bank of Fort Lee
92. U.S. Dept. of Transportation, Federal Highway Administration

93. Wisconsin Division of Veteran's Affairs
94. Union of South Africa, Dept. of Tourism
95. Mountainside Hospital
96. Western State Psychiatric Institute
97. The Motel Starlight
98. U.S. Treasury Department, Office of Internal Affairs
99. Michigan State University
100. White Rock House of Prayer

3.2 **B.** Using rough and fine sorting techniques wherever necessary, alphabetize the ten cards above.

C. On a separate sheet of paper, list the numbers on the cards in the order in which they have been arranged. Turn in your answer sheet to your teacher for checking.

D. Save these ten cards for later use.

Exercise 6

3.1 **A.** Write or type the following names in indexing order on 5 × 3 inch cards. The number beside each name should be written or typed in the upper right-hand corner of the card.

101. The Midtown Motel
102. Dinwitty County, Transportation Department
103. College of the Sacred Heart
104. Department of Health, Education, and Welfare, Division of Scholastic Loans
105. The Slumbertime Sleepnest
106. Delaware Abandoned Property Unit
107. Principality of Monaco, Bureau of Tourism
108. Mid Town National Bank
109. U.S. Dept. of Transportation, Federal Aviation Administration
110. Dominican Republic, Treasury Dept.

3.2 **B.** Using rough and fine sorting techniques wherever necessary, alphabetize the ten cards above.

C. On a separate sheet of paper, list the number on the cards in the order in which they have been arranged. Turn in your answer sheet to your teacher for checking.

D. Save these ten cards for later use.

Exercise 7

3.1 **A.** Write or type the following names in indexing order on 5 × 3 inch cards. The number beside each name should be written or typed in the upper right-hand corner of the card.

111. Deltaville Savings & Loan
112. Shalom Synagogue

113. United Arab Republic, Diplomatic Embassy
114. Stanislaus County Credit Union
115. St. Cassian's Mission
116. U.S. Dept. of Justice, Land and National Resources
117. John B. Dey Elementary School
118. Delaware Dept. of Audit & Control
119. The Sleephaven Hotel
120. Delaware State Library

3.2 **B.** Using rough and fine sorting techniques wherever necessary, alphabetize the ten cards above.

C. On a separate sheet of paper, list the numbers on the cards in the order in which they have been arranged. Turn in your answer sheet to your teacher for checking.

D. Save these ten cards for later use.

Varying the Indexing Rules

3.3 The twenty-five indexing rules you have just learned are used by most businesses and organizations in the United States. Often, in order to meet special needs of a business or organization, a rule might be varied. For example, if your company did business with a large number of banks, you might want to index them all under the city names. Or, if your company dealt with a large number of firms that have similar names, these names might be indexed under the name of the city in which they are located. Obviously, this can be a very efficient practice for the business or organization. However, *all* employees should be informed of the variation. Variations should be kept to the absolute minimum to avoid confusion. Everyone who works with files should adopt the variation.

Cross-Referencing

3.4 Always file records under the caption by which they are most likely to be requested. However, sometimes a record could be requested by a caption different from the one under which it is filed. For example, let us say you receive a letter from Stuart and Reingold, Architects, in regard to a building your company is constructing for Charles L. Wilson. When filing the letter, you decide that the letter will be requested under the name, *Stuart and Reingold, Architects,* and you file it accordingly. Because that same letter could be requested under the name, *Charles L. Wilson,* you prepare a cross-reference card or sheet and file it under *Wilson, Charles L.* This procedure is called *cross-referencing* and is much like the cross-referencing explained on page 20 in Chapter 2 of this text.

The following examples will explain when and how you should cross-reference captions.

1. As you learned in Rule 9, in indexing the name of a firm or institution not containing the full name of an individual, you consider it in the order in which it is written. However, when some word other than the first word clearly identifies the organization, use a cross-reference.

Filed Under	Cross-Reference
Society of Immigrant Workers	Immigrant Workers, Society of

2. There are many organizations in the United States today that are better known by their initials than their complete names. Records, however, should be filed according to the complete name with a cross-reference to the abbreviation.

Filed Under	Cross-Reference
American Automobile Association	AAA
American Management Association	AMA
American Medical Association	AMA
Association of Records Managers and Administrators	ARMA

3. Some records that are usually filed under their subject captions are occasionally requested by name of individual or company. In this case, the record should be filed under the subject caption with a cross-reference to the individual's or company's name.

Filed Under	Cross-Reference
Liability Insurance	MacNamara's Insurance Agency

◆ FILING PRACTICE

3.5
3.6 Complete Exercises 8 through 12 below and/or Jobs 20 through 24 in the *Progressive Filing Practice Set,* if you are using it.

Exercise 8

3.1 **A.** Arrange cards 51 through 120 in numeric order (**Example:** 51, 52, 53, 54, and so on).

3.2
3.4 **B.** Alphabetize those seventy cards using rough and fine sorting techniques wherever necessary. At the same time, cross-reference the following names:

1. Whitten & Minnetree Electronics Co., card 60; cross-reference under *Minnetree, Darrell B.,* card 60x.

2. Sampson & Hewitt Mfg. Co., card 62; cross-reference under *James H. Hewitt,* card 62x.
3. McArthur & Whiten Insurance Co., Inc., card 66; cross-reference under *George Whiten,* card 66x.
4. Walla Walla Salt Water Fishermen's Association, card 77; cross-reference under *Salt Water Fishermen's Association, Walla Walla,* card 77x.
5. Montague's Desks & Office Equipment, card 84; cross-reference under *Desks & Office Equipment, Montague's,* card 84x.
6. Minneapolis and St. Paul Coliseum, card 89; cross-reference under *St. Paul and Minneapolis Coliseum,* card 89x.

Note: The cross-reference cards will, of course, be placed where the first unit of the name on the card occurs in the alphabet.

C. On a separate sheet of paper, list the numbers on the cards in the order in which they have been arranged, including the cross-reference cards where they occur. Turn in your answer sheet to your teacher for checking.

D. Leave the cards as you have arranged them here for use in Exercise 9.

Exercise 9

3.2 **A.** With cards 51 through 120 alphabetized as in Exercise 8, as fast as possible, find the cards listed below.

> 77 Foods, Inc.
> Hot Springs Lodge
> Delaware Dept. of Audit & Control
> College of the Sacred Heart
> White Rock House of Prayer
> Dee Dee Service Station
> Hewitt Automotive Supply, Portland, Oregon
> The Sleephaven Hotel
> Michigan State University
> U.S. Dept. of Transportation, Federal Highway Administration

B. On a sheet of paper, write the names and card numbers in four columns similar to the way it has been done in the illustration beside Exercise 7 in Chapter 2. Hand in this answer sheet for checking.

Exercise 10

3.1 **A.** Write or type the following names in indexing order on 5 × 3 inch cards. The number beside each name should be written or typed in the upper right-hand corner of the card.

121. Whittaker Furniture
122. Gilbert Mott
123. Harken's Hamburger Heaven

124. Hartley's Children's Wear
125. MacDuff & McArthur, Attorneys at Law
126. San Antonio Refinery
127. Westover Hair Products
128. Barbara Martindale, M.D.
129. W O W Cheerleading Supplies
130. Williamsburg, Dept. of Child Welfare
131. Weaver's Furs, 2010 Harrison Ave.
132. Arthur Ray Hewitt
133. 16-Candles Party Service
134. D. Victoria Miltenburg
135. Debutante Delights, Ltd.
136. Sarah R. Winston
137. C. E. Winston Insulating, Inc.
138. Baxter Dasewell
139. The Wonderful World of Wax & Wicks
140. Clarence P. Whitten
141. Manford Montclair
142. A. Roberta Daniel
143. Yolanda Slayden
144. Lucien Miller
145. Seven Leaves Florists
146. Iola C. McArthur
147. Mary Beth Holly
148. Doreen Harcum
149. Maria Rosa Weaver
150. Claudia Whitten

3.2 **B.** Using rough and fine sorting techniques wherever necessary, alphabetize the thirty cards above.

C. On a separate sheet of paper, list the numbers on the cards in the order in which they have been arranged. Turn in your answer sheet to your teacher for checking.

D. Save these cards for later use.

Exercise 11
A. Combine cards 1 through 50 and the four cross-reference cards that were used in Chapter 2 with cards 51 through 150 and the six cross-reference cards that were used in this chapter. Arrange all 150 cards and 10 cross-reference cards in numeric order (**Example:** 1, 2, 3, 4, and so on).

3.4 **B.** Prepare two additional cross-reference cards for the following:

1. Baxter Dasewell, card 138; cross-reference under *Dasewell Baxter,* card 138x.
2. MacDuff & McArthur, Attorneys-at-Law, card 125; cross-reference under *McArthur & MacDuff, Attorneys-at-Law,* card 125x.

Note: The cross-reference cards will, of course, be placed where the first unit of the name on the card occurs in the alphabet.

3.2
3.4
C. Alphabetize the 150 cards and 12 cross-reference cards using rough and fine sorting techniques wherever necessary.

D. On a separate sheet of paper, list the numbers on the cards and cross-reference cards in the order in which they have been arranged. Turn in your answer sheet to your teacher for checking. Leave the cards as you have arranged them here for use in Exercise 12.

Exercise 12

3.2
A. Using the cards that were alphabetized in Exercise 11, find the cards listed below as fast as possible.

Lucien B. Miller	Alberta P. Daswell
Marie-Caroline Sanipy	J. Widdons
Bron E. Milter	Harold Danielson
Harold Sampson	Irving MacDuff, Jr.
7th Avenue Disco	Weaver's Furs,
Dial a Steak	2208 Fifth Avenue
St. Petersburg Brewery	Million-Seller Records
Arthur U. Hewitt	77 Foods, Inc.
Stuart Michael	Douglas Harcum
Meena-Arjan	Harold Samuel
Imports-Exports, Ltd.	Downtown Restaurant

B. On a sheet of paper, write the names and card numbers in four columns similar to the way it has been done in the illustration beside exercise 7 in Chapter 2. Hand in this answer sheet for checking.

◆ HAVE YOU MET YOUR COMPETENCIES?

3.1
3.2
Have you successfully completed Exercises 1 through 12 in this chapter?

3.3
State an example in which an indexing rule might be varied or changed in order to meet the needs of a special business situation.

3.4
Have you successfully completed the cross-reference part of Exercise 8 and Exercise 11 in this chapter?

3.5
3.6
Have you successfully completed Jobs 9 through 24 in the *Progressive Filing Practice Set?*

Chapter

4

Organizing
Alphabetic
Correspondence
Files

Competencies

4.1   Define *correspondence* as it applies to filing.

4.2   Give three advantages of using alphabetic correspondence filing in business.

4.3   Define *guide, guide rod, caption, tab, position, cut, folder* (*individual* and *miscellaneous*), and *expansion scores.*

4.4   Type file folder labels for use in alphabetic correspondence files.

4.5   Given unarranged guides, individual folders, and miscellaneous folders, list them in the order in which they would appear in a file drawer.

4.6   Identify three types of equipment used to file correspondence alphabetically.

Correspondence Filing

4.1 Businesses cannot function without written communications both in their in-company operations and in their dealings with outside organizations and firms. These written communications are in the form of letters, mailgrams, orders, invoices, checks, bills, reports, and other miscellaneous papers. If you were to look up the word *correspondence* in the dictionary, you would see that *correspondence* usually refers to letters only. However, for the purpose of filing, we will consider correspondence to be all of the written communications mentioned above. We will use this overall definition of the word *correspondence* to distinguish the filing of correspondence from the filing of cards.

Most companies file correspondence *vertically,* or on edge. It is faster and easier to file vertically because papers can be handled independently.

The filing and finding of cards involves the application of the basic indexing rules to the name on the card. Correspondence filing, however, involves a number of other decisions. Each piece of correspondence generally has more than one name on it, so your first task is to determine under which name it should be filed. When you have selected that name, your next job is to apply the basic indexing rules. And last, since the piece of correspondence will be placed with other papers stored under the same caption, you must file the correspondence in proper sequence within those other papers. Hence we can say that *vertical correspondence filing* is the bringing together in one place of all correspondence to, from, or about one individual, one firm, one place, or one subject. These records are placed on edge, generally in folders behind guides. This method of filing ensures speed, accuracy, and accessibility.

Alphabetic Correspondence Filing

4.2 Many businesses file correspondence alphabetically. For example, any business with a great deal of incoming and outgoing correspondence would find it advantageous to have an alphabetic correspondence file. Needless to say, such a file is based on a sequence with which everyone is familiar—the *alphabet.* Aside from that, it is *direct;* in other words, records can be stored immediately without referring to another index or file to obtain information. An alphabetic correspondence file is also *flexible.* Any number of divisions can be made. For example, a small firm or organization may simply have guides for each letter of the alphabet: *A, B, C, D,* and so on. A larger firm or organization could further subdivide those captions by breaking down each letter: *B, Be, Bi, Bo, Br,* and even *Bro.*

Alphabetic correspondence filing procedures, terms, and materials often apply to other methods of filing, such as subject, numeric, or geographic filing.

Chapter 4. Organizing Alphabetic Correspondence Files

4.3 *Guides* are generally made of heavy cardboard or pressboard and are slightly larger than the records to be filed. Guides perform two basic functions: (1) they act as "signposts" to guide the file worker's eye quickly to the places desired within the file; and (2) they provide support for the records that are contained within the file.

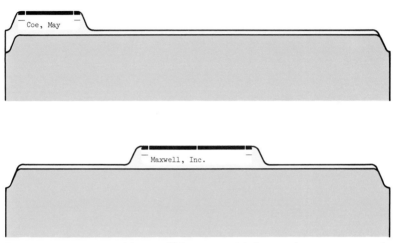

Folders and guides with one-fifth or one-third cut tabs are commonly used in offices.

The standard vertical file drawer (about 26 inches in depth) has a maximum capacity of 5,000 pieces of paper; this includes the necessary guides and folders. If the drawer were used to capacity, there would be little operating space. For more efficient use, the maximum number should be about 4,000 pieces. The usual number of guides in a file drawer ranges between 20 and 40. Guides provide support as well as proper distribution of papers, which facilitates easy reference. The number of guides used is generally determined by the type of office. Printed guide captions may be purchased, or the guide captions may be prepared in the office. These printed guides are made in various divisions of the alphabet. They range in size from sets of 26 guides for small offices to sets of 200,000 guides for very large organizations.

Guide Rods. Guides usually are equipped with a projection at the bottom center that contains a metal-reinforced hole in the middle. The *guide rod,* which is a metal rod included in most file drawers, is placed through those holes in the bottom of the guides to hold them in place within the file drawer.

Captions

4.3 The titles on the guide tabs are called *captions*. Captions should be short so that they can be read easily and quickly on the guides. A *single caption* means that only one letter or one combination of letters appears on a guide tab. The names to be filed *after* any guide should begin *only* with the caption printed on that guide tab and go up to—but *not* include— the caption printed on the next guide tab.

Double, or *closed,* captions indicate not only where a section of the file starts but also where it ends. Sometimes these double captions appear side by side and are separated by a hyphen, such as *B-Be, Bi-Bo,* as shown in the illustration. Sometimes these captions appear one below the other.

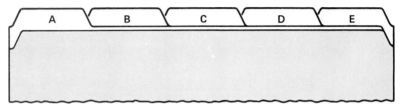

One-fifth cut staggered guides with single captions.

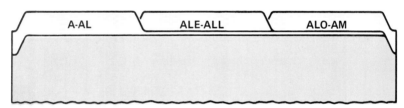

One-third cut staggered guides with double captions.

Single captions are the most flexible since they can be expanded easily. Additional guides can be inserted wherever they are needed. Needless to say, single captions permit larger type and the letters on the tabs are easy to read. In order for a file worker to determine what records appear behind a single caption, the next caption must be seen. Double captions have the advantage of telling the file worker exactly what alphabetic range is covered by the guide.

Tabs, Positions, and Cuts

4.3 Captions appear on the *tab,* or extended portion of the upper edge of a guide or folder. Tabs may appear in various places, called *positions,* along the top edge of the guide, or the back edge of the folder. These positions are identified by the place in which they occur, reading from left to right. When a tab is one-fifth cut and placed at the extreme left of the upper edge, the guide (or folder) is called *one-fifth cut, first position*. This is because the tabs are made in various widths, known as *cuts*. The one-fifth cut is so called because the tab occupies one-fifth of the space on the upper edge. If the tab occupied one-third of the space on the edge of the guide, it would be called one-third cut. When a tab is one-third cut and placed in the center of the upper edge, the guide is termed *one-third cut, center position*. Guides are said to be in *staggered arrangement* when the tabs occupy all positions from left to right in the file drawer.

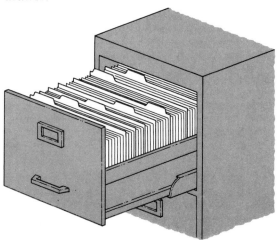

The staggered arrangement makes the guides easy to locate.

Folders

Many different kinds of folders are available that are designed for different filing needs. The most common folder is the manila folder. It comes in several weights and has straight edges or tabs in various positions. Another frequently used folder is the hanging folder that is suspended from a metal frame inside the file drawer. Folders designed for special needs include envelope folders, which are useful when records must be carried often from place to place, and folders with adjustable signals, which are useful for papers that need to be followed up. Open-shelf files sometimes require special folders and guides with tabs on the side end rather than at the top.

4.3   When there are five or more records from one correspondent, an *individual folder* is opened for that correspondent. Fewer than five records from any correspondent during a filing period (from six months to two years) are stored in a *miscellaneous folder*. Remember, an individual folder contains records from only one correspondent; a miscellaneous folder contains records from one or a great many correspondents.

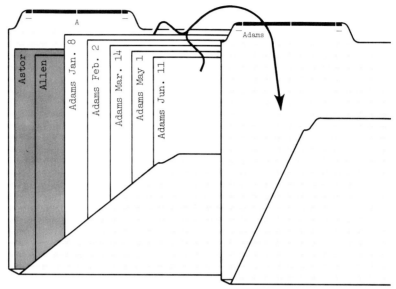

Since there are five Adams letters, an individual folder is opened for *Adams.* Other papers indexed under *A* remain in the miscellaneous *A* folder.

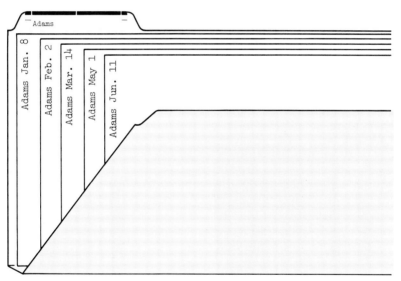

Papers in individual folders should be filed with the latest date in front.

Individual Folders

4.3 Since records are usually requested by date as well as by name, they should be arranged chronologically within an individual folder, with the latest date in front. In some companies, records are requested by location or by subject as well as by name. In this case, they should not be arranged by date, but rather in an order that permits fast finding.

The Adams records are now separated by year because there are a great many of them.

When the number of records for one individual or firm reaches 100, the records should be divided—either by date, location, or subject—and another individual folder should be opened.

Miscellaneous Folders

Unless you are aware ahead of time that more than five records will accumulate for one correspondent or subject during a filing period, the first record relating to this correspondent or subject should be stored in the miscellaneous, or group, folder. This group folder should carry the same caption as the preceding guide. The folder will temporarily hold correspondence that does not warrant an individual folder.

Because the miscellaneous folder contains records pertaining to a variety of names or subjects, records should be arranged alphabetically within the folder. When there are two or more records pertaining to the same correspondent or subject, arrange those records by date, or chronologically, with the latest date in front.

Typing File Folder Labels

4.4   File folder labels are available in various styles and colors. Most labels are about 4 inches wide. They may be set up on 8½- by 11-inch sheets that have perforations to separate the labels, on adhesive strips, or in continuous rolls. Some labels are self-sticking and need no moistening; other labels are gummed and must be moistened before application.

Hanging folders are constructed so that the label is inserted in a clear plastic tab that is positioned in slots at the top of the folder. Labels for hanging folders come in perforated strips without glue since they are held in place by the plastic tab.

Follow these suggestions when you type folder labels:

1. Begin each caption in the same position so that all captions will be in a straight line in the file drawer. For most labels, start the caption on the third space in from the left edge and on the second line below the top edge.
2. Type the words or items of the caption in indexing order. (**Example:** *Mason, Linda M.,* not *Linda M. Mason.*)

4.4 **3.** Adhere to the basic typing style for the captions already in use in your employer's files. Some businesses prefer to type the first word of the caption in all caps with the remaining words in upper and lower case. (**Example:** *MASON, Linda M.*) However, most offices type the caption as it appears in Item 2 of this list.

     4. Check the punctuation style already in use in your employer's files. Some offices choose to omit punctuation entirely, including the periods after abbreviations. Instead, they leave two spaces where the punctuation would have been. However, most offices use standard punctuation. Adhere to the style already in use.

     5. If more than one item is included in the caption, block style is generally preferred. If the caption runs over to another line, the second line is generally indented three spaces. Check the style used by your employer and follow that procedure.

4.5 **6.** Arrange folders by captions in alphabetic order following the procedure explained in Rules 1 and 2 (page 11).

Arranging Alphabetic Guides and Folders

4.6 Correspondence is usually filed in vertical or lateral file cabinets. A vertical cabinet has from two to five drawers; the cabinet is tall, narrow, and deep. A lateral file cabinet has two or three drawers; this cabinet is short, wide, and not as deep as the vertical cabinet. The lateral cabinet is becoming more and more widely used since it does not take up as much office space or aisle space as the vertical cabinet. Also, it is easier to reach the back of a drawer in a lateral cabinet than in a vertical one.

For storing papers that are needed for everyday reference, or for storing everyday supplies, desk workers use the desk file drawer.

Whatever type of file cabinet is used, a systematic arrangement of guides and folders is necessary for efficient storage and retrieval.

The order of guides and folders for a given caption in the file drawer is as follows: (1) guide, (2) individual folders, and (3) miscellaneous folder.

When storing records in the file, the office worker must first locate the proper guide and then look over the individual folders that follow the guide. If no individual folder exists for a particular name or subject, the worker places the correspondence in the miscellaneous folder. The miscellaneous folder is placed *after* the individual folders. This prevents filing errors and lost motion because the motion always goes toward the *back* of the file drawer. If the miscellaneous folder had been placed in front of the individual folders, the worker might make the mistake of storing the papers in the miscellaneous folders when, in fact, there was an individual folder for the person or subject.

There should be from five to ten individual folders behind any one guide. If the drawer contains only miscellaneous folders, the number of folders behind any one guide should not exceed five.

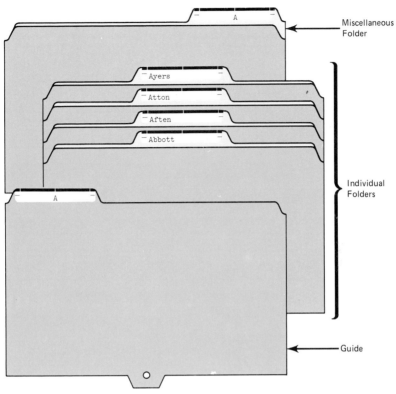

In actual practice, there would probably be more than four folders behind any one guide.

◆ HAVE YOU MET YOUR COMPETENCIES?

4.1 Define *correspondence* as it applies to filing.

4.2 Give three advantages of using alphabetic correspondence filing in business.

4.3 Define the following:

guide	cut
guide rod	folder
caption	individual folder
tab	miscellaneous folder
position	expansion scores

4.4 If you have the *Progressive Filing Practice Set,* you should now refer to your *Practice Instruction Manual* to complete Job 25. Otherwise, complete the following exercise.

Type the following information on folder labels for an alphabetic correspondence file. If folders are available, attach the labels to them.

4.4   Ralston's Cooking School
       Reynolds Memorial Hospital
       Seafood Cookware, Inc.
       Slodysko-Sloan
       Table Kettle Kitchenware
       Town & County Rental Service
       U.S. Government Resale Service Office
       Upton's Kitchen Ware, Inc.
       Van de Meer & Moats, CPAs
       Vanity Tableware, Ltd.

4.5   List the guides, individual folders, and miscellaneous folders shown in the following table in the order in which they would appear in a file drawer.

Guides	Individual Folders	Miscellaneous Folders
H	E. A. Holsten, Inc.	J
J	R. H. Ingram	I
K	Lobianco & Nettleton, Inc.	L
I	K & L Plumbing and Heating	K
L	Holmes Automotive Service Co.	H
	Phillip Benjamin Lomasang	
	Long Creek Marina	
	Insurance Agency of Toledo	
	Jones-Nettleton Insurance	
	Brenda H. Judd, CPA	

4.6   Name and describe three types of equipment used to file correspondence alphabetically.

Chapter

Alphabetic
Correspondence
Filing
Procedures

Competencies

5.1 State the purpose of a time stamp.

5.2 State the purpose of a release mark.

5.3 Enumerate the steps in the filing process.

5.4 Describe these procedures: *inspecting, indexing, coding, sorting, storing, retrieval, charging out,* and *creating a new folder.*

5.5 Given an illustration of a section of an alphabetic correspondence file and the name of a document to be located, state where you would first look to locate the document. State other locations where the same document might be found if it were misfiled.

5.6 Given a miniature alphabetic correspondence file and miniature correspondence, perform the procedures necessary to file, cross-reference, find, and charge-out correspondence. (See Jobs 26 through 31 in the *Progressive Filing Practice Set.*)

A business firm may use an individual work station system for filing or a central location system, or both. The worker in charge of the files at an individual work station (such as a stenographer or a secretary) is responsible only for the papers of one or two executives. Procedures at an individual work station, therefore, may not be as formal as for central filing.

Workers in a central filing location are responsible for the records of any number of executives or departments of the company. All the important records of the company may be stored in that one location. In this case, procedures for filing and requesting records are usually strictly defined.

Steps Preliminary to Filing

Experience has shown that many records are lost or misplaced *before* they are filed. Therefore, an efficient filing system begins before records are placed in file cabinets.

A definite procedure should be established by every business for the regular, reliable collection of all records that need to be filed. This procedure should be the same regardless of the size of the organization and regardless of whether files are kept at individual work stations or in a central filing department. A large organization with mail and filing departments, each of which has many employees, or a small office that employs one or two workers should make sure that all employees responsible for filing follow a set of organized procedures for filing records.

The Time Stamp

5.1 All incoming correspondence—with the exception of personal mail—should be opened and time-stamped. In many small offices, this is done by hand; more often, however, a machine or rubber stamp is used. The stamp indicates the date so that later responsibility can be fixed for the amount of time that elapses between the day the piece of correspondence was received and the day it was answered or otherwise handled. Once the correspondence has been time-stamped, it should be delivered to the person in the company who will handle it as necessary.

Correspondence to be filed should not be allowed to pile up. Filing should be done often; hence the records to be filed should be collected at *regular* intervals. Records that are kept properly in files are safe and easy to find; records kept in desk trays or desk drawers are not.

Release Marks

5.2 In many offices, particularly where files are kept in a file department, a record must bear a *release mark* before it is filed. A *release mark* is a signal

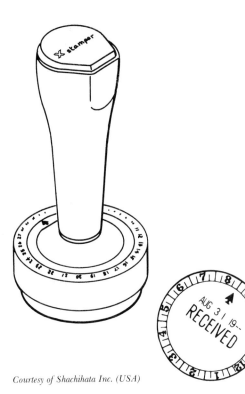

Courtesy of Shachihata Inc. (USA)

This is a common hand stamp used to record date and approximate time.

that the paper has received the necessary attention and is ready to be filed. The release mark may consist of the initials of the person releasing it, the date, or both. It may be a boss's note—"File"—on the paper. The release mark may be made with a rubber stamp or it may be handwritten; it usually appears in the upper left-hand corner of the record to be filed.

In an individual work station, releasing a paper for filing is merely a matter of the boss placing it in the "out" box for the secretary to pick up.

Whatever method is used, it is important that papers ready for filing be kept separately from those that are not. Those papers that are not ready for filing are kept on hand until they are taken care of.

Carbon copies of outgoing correspondence do not need release marks. The carbon copy shows that whatever action was required has been taken.

Steps in the Filing Process

5.3   In the vertical filing of correspondence, there are five steps: (1) inspecting, (2) indexing, (3) coding, (4) sorting, and (5) storing. These steps are illustrated on page 58.

STEPS IN CORRESPONDENCE FILING

1. INSPECTING. Correspondence is checked to make sure it has been released for filing.

2. INDEXING. The name by which correspondence will most likely be requested from the files is determined. In this example it was decided that the *Riverside National Bank* would be the caption under which the letter would be filed.

3. CODING. The caption determined in the indexing step is underscored.

   The cross-reference caption is underscored and an *X* placed at the end of the line.

4. SORTING. All correspondence to be filed is sorted in alphabetic order according to the underscored captions.

5. STORING. The papers are placed in the proper folders in the filing cabinets.

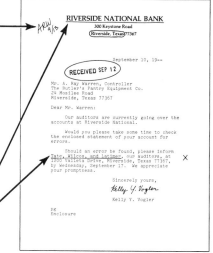

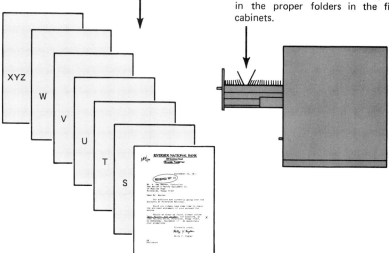

5.4 **Step 1. Inspecting.** In an office that uses release marks, the first step in the preparation of correspondence for filing is *inspecting*. Each piece must be inspected to make sure that it has been released for filing. Any piece that has no release marks should be returned to the person who worked with it.

If release marks are not used, the person who is doing the filing should make sure that the person responsible for releasing the paper for filing has finished with it.

Step 2. Indexing. The mental process of determining the name, subject, or other caption under which the correspondence is to be filed is called *indexing*. When a letter, for example, is indexed, there are five possibilities:

1. The name on the letterhead.
2. The name of the person or company to whom the letter is addressed.
3. The name in the signature.
4. The name or subject mentioned in the letter.
5. The name of a location.

When selecting a caption, the indexer must determine the most likely heading under which the correspondence will be requested from the files.

The indexer, often a stenographer or secretary, should remember that employees other than the indexer should be able to locate a record that is needed.

Whenever a record may be requested in several ways, it is filed under the most important caption and cross-referenced under the other names or subjects by which it may be requested. Remember that *cross-referencing* means either (1) placing sheets of paper containing information about the actual location of a record in all places in a file where a person might look for it or (2) placing a photocopy of the original record in all places in a file where a person might look for it.

Step 3. Coding. *Coding* is the process of marking the caption selected on the correspondence during the indexing operation. Three common methods of coding correspondence for an alphabetic system are:

1. The name selected as the caption is underlined, generally using a colored pencil, on the correspondence itself.
2. If the name or caption chosen does not appear in the record, it is written in a colored pencil in the upper right-hand corner.
3. If a record requires cross-referencing, the caption under which it is cross-referenced is also underlined or written. An X is placed at the end of the line or after the written caption to show that it is a cross-reference and not the original filing caption. (See the illustration of a coded letter on page 58.)

Not only does coding point out the indexing caption for the worker when the record is filed for the first time, but it also helps later when the record needs to be replaced after it has been borrowed from the files.

The coding step may be skipped when files are kept at individual work stations rather than in a central file department. A new employee responsible for filing at an individual work station may find it helpful to code all papers until that employee becomes familiar with the names of correspondents and topics that are filed. Once the employee is familiar with the names, scanning the paper to identify the caption is all that is necessary; underscoring or writing the caption is not done.

Step 4. Sorting. Placing records in alphabetic order according to the captions which have been underlined or written on them is called *sorting.* Arranging the papers alphabetically aids the worker by speeding up the process of placing them in the files. No matter how small the office, preliminary alphabetizing of the records saves the worker from moving back and forth from drawer to drawer while storing the papers. Opening and closing drawers and moving back and forth wastes time and energy. By sorting first, the file worker may open each drawer only once and work systematically from front to back.

Where a large number of records are filed at one time, special equipment might be used to speed up the process of sorting. The use of rubber fingertips makes papers easier to handle. Frequently, papers are simply sorted on a table or desk top.

Sorting of this type should follow these steps:

1. Sort papers into a small number of piles according to divisions, such as *A–C, D–G, H–L, M–R,* and *S–Z.*
2. Re-sort those papers in each of the five alphabetic divisions above. For example, the *A–C* pile would be redivided to three piles—one for *A*, one for *B*, and one for *C*.
3. Within those piles, alphabetize the papers. For example, the *A* pile might have papers for *Allen, Archer, Abrams,* and *Abraham.* They would be placed in alphabetic order, *Abraham, Abrams, Allen,* and *Archer,* ready to be filed.
4. Assemble all the piles alphabetically. After the *A–C* pile has been alphabetized, it may be taken to the files. The remaining divisions would then be sorted and taken to the files. If the number of records is not exceptionally large, all the records may be taken to the files at one time to be stored. Otherwise, smaller divisions might be taken.

Step 5. Storing. The fifth step in vertical correspondence filing is *storing,* or actually placing the records in a file container, such as a folder, according to some predetermined plan.

Once the file worker locates the folder, the caption on the folder should be carefully checked to see that it matches the name underscored on the record and the name coded on the first record already in the folder. The eye generally catches underscores and misfiling records will be prevented.

If papers are not coded, the paper should be checked by quickly scanning it to make sure it belongs in the folder.

Once the file worker is sure that the folder is the correct one, the folder should be raised and rested on the side of the drawer before papers are placed in it. This helps in placing the records evenly and quickly at the bottom of the folder as well as further ensuring that the folder is the correct one.

Regardless of the size of the record, it should be placed in the file folder with the heading to the left as you face the file. Never overcrowd folders. Most folders hold 100 pieces of correspondence, but it is better to subdivide records before they reach full capacity. Otherwise, the records will "ride up" in the folder and hide the label.

THE STORAGE OF CORRESPONDENCE IN A DRAWER FILE

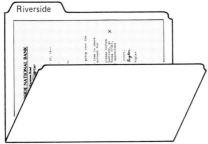

1. Locate the proper folder. Lift and rest it on the side of the drawer.

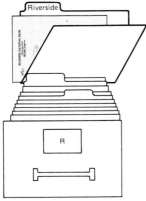

2. Compare the caption on the record to be filed with the caption on the record in the folder.

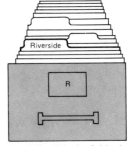

3. Place the record in the folder with the letterhead to the left.

4. Carefully slide the folder back to original position. Close the drawer.

Managing the Files

Once records are stored, the purpose of any filing system—to store information so that it is easily located when needed—is put to the test.

Retrieval. Locating and removing records from the files is called *retrieval.* The five steps in filing that you have just studied are important for efficient retrieval.

5.4   In the second step, indexing—when you determine the caption under which to file a record—always keep in mind ease of retrieval and cross-reference wherever cross-referencing will aid in finding a record. If a record may be called for by more than one name or subject, the additional names or subjects should be cross-referenced to speed the location of the paper.

Charge-Out System. The procedure used to request and account for records removed from the files is called *charging-out.* This procedure applies primarily to centralized files, but it may apply in a less formal way to individual work station files. Also, the records might be removed from the files for use by someone else in the organization.

Good records management calls for a control system that accounts for all records whether they are in the files or being used. This system, no matter what size the organization, would indicate what records are out, who has them, when they were borrowed, and when they will be returned. In any control, or *charge-out,* system, there are generally three steps.

1. Requests for filed material must be handled.
2. The material must be charged to the person or persons who requested it.
3. The material must be followed up to be sure it is returned to the files.

The amount of clerical work necessary in the charge-out system will be determined by whether the files are kept at individual work stations or in a central file department. In a filing department, the system would be much more elaborate than for individual work station files.

Requesting Records From the Files. There are several ways in which a record might be requested from the files—by telephone, by messenger, or by the personal appearance of the office worker requesting the record. Whenever possible, records should be requested *in writing* and a standard requisition form should be used. Any oral requests should be recorded on this standard form as soon as they are received. Requisition slips may be printed, duplicated, or purchased.

There are a number of items that every requisition slip should include: (1) the borrower's signature (not just the name); (2) the borrower's name (if the signature is not readable); (3) what the requested record is about; (4) the date the record is borrowed; (5) the date the record is to be returned; (6) the date of the record itself; and (7) the department in which the person requesting the record is employed.

If the record is returned to the files immediately, a requisition slip is often unnecessary. In small offices, where requests are usually received orally or where the borrower obtains the records from the files, the requisition slip is often unnecessary. If the records are not to

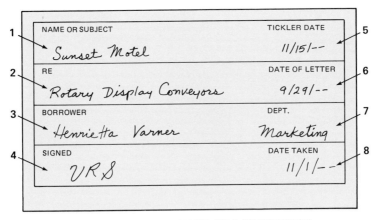

NAME OR SUBJECT	TICKLER DATE
Sunset Motel	11/15/--
RE	DATE OF LETTER
Rotary Display Conveyors	9/29/--
BORROWER	DEPT.
Henrietta Varner	*Marketing*
SIGNED	DATE TAKEN
VRS	11/1/--

INFORMATION CONTAINED ON A REQUISITION

1. The name indexed on the borrowed record.
2. What the record is about or regarding.
3. The name of the borrower.
4. The name of the person who obtained the record.

5. The date the record is to be returned.
6. The date of the record.
7. The borrower's department.
8. The date the record was borrowed.

be returned to the files immediately, a requisition slip should be made out. This is the basis for the second step of the charge-out procedure: the material must be charged to the person or persons who requested it. This step makes the borrower responsible for the return of the records.

Charging Out Records. When records are charged out, a notation should be made in the files. This notation indicates who has the records. Such a notation is usually made in one of three ways: by *out guides,* by *out folders,* or by *substitution cards.* Out guides are made of the same heavy cardboard used for the filing location guides. There are basically two types of "out" guides: (1) the pocket type, which allows the requisition slip to be placed in that pocket, or (2) a type without the pocket, which permits a cumulative list that provides a history of how the records have been used and by whom. Out guides and out folders are used when an entire folder is removed from the files. An out folder, which is generally preferred to out guides, provides a folder for any new records that need to be filed while the original folder is out of the files. The front of an out folder has a place for information similar to that written on a cumulative out guide.

Often, when an entire folder is needed, a *carrier folder* is used for the borrowed pages, and the file folder is kept in place. These special carrier folders are made of a heavy material so that they can stand the wear and tear of a great deal of handling. Generally, they have a distinctive color that helps to avoid their loss and to speed their return to the files.

Even though these charge-out forms differ in size and make-up, each one contains:
1. The name indexed on the borrowed record;   2. The date of the record;   3. The name of the borrower;   4. The date the record was borrowed;   5. The date the record is to be returned (follow-up date).

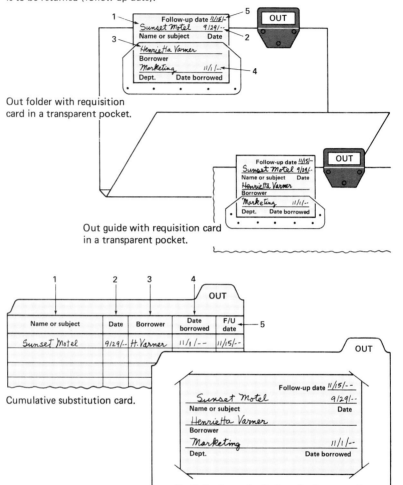

Out folder with requisition card in a transparent pocket.

Out guide with requisition card in a transparent pocket.

Cumulative substitution card.

Substitution card with requisition card attached.

5.4   Substitution cards, like out guides, may be either the pocket type or the cumulative type. Substitution cards are used when one or several records are removed from a folder. Like carrier folders, substitution cards are usually of a distinctive color so that they can be inserted in the regular folder to indicate the removal of a specific record.

When one record must be circulated among a number of people or departments, the following two timesaving methods may be used.

1. Each person, when finished with the record, passes it on to the next person, and fills out a transfer slip that is sent to the filing department. The file worker uses that slip as the basis for recharging the out guide.
2. Names of all persons to use the record are listed on it, and each name is checked off by the user after it has been given the necessary attention. The user then passes the material on to the next person on the list. A duplicate copy of the list is kept with the out guide, so the record can be traced if necessary.

As papers are returned to the files, the substitution card, out guide, or out folder should be removed and the charge-out notation on it marked off. A supply of substitution cards, out guides, and out folders should be kept in the front or back of every file drawer for convenience.

Following Up Borrowed Records. Your job may include following up borrowed records; that is, making sure that each record is returned to the files on the due date. The length of time for which papers may be kept depends on the particular office. Certain valuable or confidential papers may have to be returned to the files before the end of the day. Others may be kept longer. Whatever the case, the file worker should set aside a definite time to check charge-outs and to trace records that have been out longer than the allowed loan period. The longer these records stay out of the files, the more apt they are to be misplaced. Anyone who is responsible for files should establish follow-up procedures. These procedures will reduce the number of lost records.

Where there are few file drawers to check, it is a simple matter for the person responsible for the files to check the due dates on borrowed records from the substitution cards, out guides, or out folders in the file drawers. Where there are many file drawers to check, a desk *tickler file* is used.

A tickler file is a follow-up file that is usually organized by date. The tickler file system works in this way. A record is charged out and a requisition card is inserted in the pocket of an out guide or is attached to a substitution card. Then a duplicate copy of the requisition card is placed in the tickler file behind the date on which the borrowed record is to be returned to the files.

Regardless of the follow-up system used, the person responsible for the files checks each day to determine what records are due and notifies the borrower. If the borrower still needs the records, the due date is extended. The requisition card that is placed in the out guide or attached to the substitution card is changed accordingly, as is the duplicate card that is placed in the tickler file. Otherwise, the records are returned and the charge is canceled.

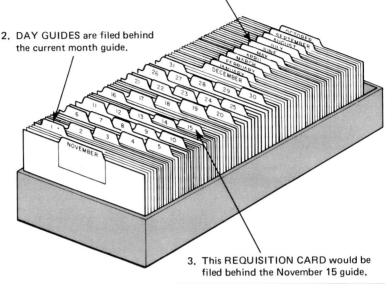

1. All MONTH GUIDES except the current month guide are stored behind the day guides.

2. DAY GUIDES are filed behind the current month guide.

3. This REQUISITION CARD would be filed behind the November 15 guide.

NAME OR SUBJECT	TICKLER DATE
Sunset Motel	11/15/--
RE	DATE OF LETTER
Rotary Display Conveyors	9/29/--
BORROWER	DEPT.
Henrietta Varner	Marketing
SIGNED	DATE TAKEN
VRS	11/1/--

5.4   It is not unusual for a file department to receive a request for records to be delivered at some future date. Such a request can also be placed in the tickler file behind the proper date. If there is a large number of advance requests, two tickler files might be necessary: one for follow-up and one for advance requests.

Creating a New File Folder

If you are responsible for maintaining files, it may be your job to check miscellaneous folders to see if there are five or more records for one correspondent. If so, it is your job to create a new file folder for that individual. You might also need to open a new file folder when the capacity of an existing folder has been reached.

5.5 If all file workers follow the correct procedures for using and maintaining files, needed records should be found easily and quickly. Sometimes, however, a record is misfiled. If you are responsible for conducting a search for that misfiled document, there are a number of steps that can be followed to locate the missing record.

1. See if the record is out of order in the folder where it should be filed.
2. Check desk trays where it might be found.
3. Look in the folders directly in front of and directly behind the folder in which the record should be filed.
4. Look in the space in front of, behind, and under the proper folder.
5. In an alphabetic filing system, look under names that have a similar spelling or sound. (**Example:** *Homes* for *Holmes.*)
6. In an alphabetic system, try the other indexing units of the missing record. (**Example:** *Minneapolis Department of Parks*—check *Parks* and check *Department.*)
7. Look under names or subjects that are related in some way to the missing record. (**Example:** *Minneapolis Department of Parks*—check *City of Minneapolis;* check *Minnesota.*)
8. In a numeric system, try every possible arrangement of the correct folder number. (**Example:** If the correct folder number is *4903,* check under *9403, 4093, 4039, 4309,* and so on.)

Even in the most efficiently managed files, mistakes can occur. If a record is not where it should be, the worker should not become upset, but should organize a search as is described and illustrated here. If the missing record is located, the file worker should then take steps to eliminate the possibility of a similar loss in the future. If the record is not located, a copy of the missing record should be inserted in the file, or its loss should be made known to other employees so that needless searches will not be made again.

There are several guidelines that help to eliminate the loss of records:

1. When placing sorted records in the files, the file worker should stand at the side of the drawer. From the side position, rather than the front, the worker does not have to reach as far.
2. Proper lighting in the filing department or area can prevent misfiling records.
3. The file worker should always pull up any folder in which records are to be stored. This procedure will prevent records from slipping between folders or falling to the bottom of the drawer where they may be lost.

HOW TO CONDUCT AN ORGANIZED SEARCH FOR A LOST RECORD

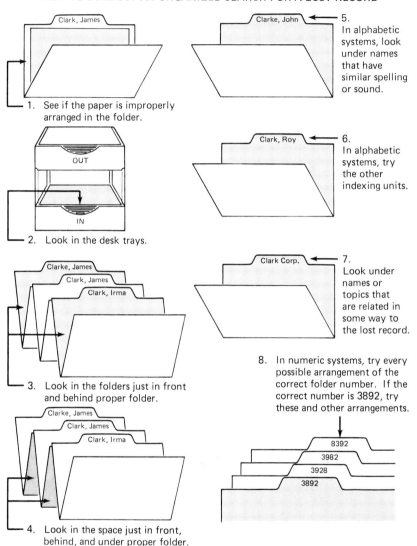

1. See if the paper is improperly arranged in the folder.

2. Look in the desk trays.

3. Look in the folders just in front and behind proper folder.

4. Look in the space just in front, behind, and under proper folder.

5. In alphabetic systems, look under names that have similar spelling or sound.

6. In alphabetic systems, try the other indexing units.

7. Look under names or topics that are related in some way to the lost record.

8. In numeric systems, try every possible arrangement of the correct folder number. If the correct number is 3892, try these and other arrangements.

4. The use of paper clips in the files should be avoided. Although they conveniently hold together records that must be grouped, they will latch onto records that are not related. Paper clips also add to the bulk of a file folder. Staples are preferred to paper clips within the files.

5. Each time a record or folder is to be returned to a file drawer *immediately*, the worker should slightly lift or raise the record or folder behind the one removed in order to make it easier to return the record or folder to its proper position. (Of course, if the record or folder is

not to be returned immediately, an out guide, folder, or card should be used.)

◆ HAVE YOU MET YOUR COMPETENCIES?

5.1 State the purpose of a time stamp.

5.2 State the purpose of a release mark.

5.3 Enumerate the steps in the filing process.

5.4 Describe these procedures:

inspecting	storing
indexing	retrieval
coding	charging out
sorting	creating a new folder

5.5 You have been asked to locate the following document: a letter from Jeffrey E. Batt to your employer explaining a national survey. In the file illustrated below, where would you look for this document?

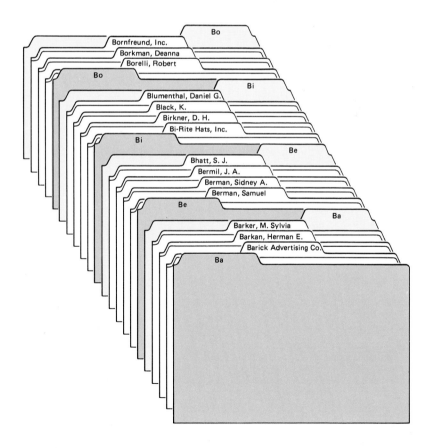

5.5 If this document were not located there, what other places would you look to locate this misfiled document?

5.6 If you have the *Progressive Filing Practice Set,* you should now refer to your *Practice Instruction Manual* for instructions to complete Jobs 26 through 31.

Chapter

Subject
Correspondence
Filing
Procedures

Competencies

6.1 Give two examples in which subject correspondence filing would be used.

6.2 Arrange captions on guides and folders in order for a subject correspondence file.

6.3 List and describe the steps to be followed in subject correspondence filing.

6.4 Describe the three kinds of subject files.

6.5 Given brief statements of the contents of correspondence and a listing of the captions, assign a subject caption to each statement.

6.6 State the advantages of a planned transfer and retention procedure.

6.7 State two or more methods used in transferring documents from active to inactive status.

6.8 Perform the procedures necessary to file and cross-reference correspondence in an alphabetic subject system. (See Jobs 32 through 34 in the *Progressive Filing Practice Set.*)

6.9 Transfer selected items in an alphabetic subject correspondence file to inactive status. (See Job 35 in the *Progressive Filing Practice Set.*)

6.10 Perform the procedures necessary to file, cross-reference, and find correspondence in a numeric subject system. (See Jobs 36 through 39 in the *Progressive Filing Practice Set.*)

Subject Files

6.1 It is often more efficient for a business to file by subject rather than alphabetically. This simply means that records are arranged by *topic* or *thing* rather than by letters of the alphabet according to the names of people or companies. The yellow pages of your telephone book are arranged by subject. This arrangement makes it possible to look for a company according to the type of goods or kind of services that the company provides.

Just as a definite routine should be followed for alphabetic correspondence filing, an established procedure should be used for subject correspondence filing.

Many businesses use subject correspondence filing. For example, an office machine company might have files arranged according to the types of machines they sell, like this: *Adding Machines, Addressing Machines, Calculating Machines, Copiers, Duplicating Machines,* and so on. Most often these files would be used for one of the following objectives:

1. **To organize records that do not refer to the name of a person or organization.** A drug company might file chemical formulas according to the drug for which the formula is used.

2. **To organize correspondence that is more likely to be called for by its subject than by the name of the correspondent.** An insurance policy covering the office furniture, for example, might be asked for as "our office furniture insurance policy," rather than as "policy number 2J77428," or "The Mutual Insurance Company policy." The policy would therefore best be filed under the subject heading *Insurance—Office Furniture.*

3. **To group records concerning the activities or products of an organization (such as advertising and sales, or typewriters and adding machines) so that all the records about one activity or product can be obtained immediately from the files.** (If you are using the *Progressive Filing Practice Set,* you will notice that The Butler's Pantry Equipment Company has subject filing captions for the various products that they sell and distribute. For example, if a customer requires information about a particular type of conveyor, it is possible to go to the files and look for the information under *conveyors* rather than checking with the manufacturers of the various types of conveyors. If the information were scattered about under the names of the various manufacturers, the search for information would be a lengthy one.)

4. **To group together records that would otherwise fall into minute subdivisions.** For example, a large furniture dealer might purchase products from hundreds of different suppliers. The volume of correspondence from individual suppliers might be small. This could create files that would be cumbersome because of the hundreds of names that would

have to be kept in an alphabetic correspondence file. With subject filing, however, the dealer could organize files on a product basis with only a dozen or so major headings. Correspondence would be filed according to product, and only an alphabetic card index would be needed to maintain a list of suppliers and the products they sell.

The Organization of a Subject File

Because subject files must meet the requirements of each individual business, it is highly unlikely that any two subject files would ever be organized in the same manner. As an example, let's look at the files for a public vocational school that accepts students from five public high schools and several private schools.

This vocational school is located in a large metropolitan area. It has approximately 1,100 students, 30 faculty members, 2 administrators, as well as an office staff, custodians, and cafeteria workers. The school is part of an 8,000-employee school system. In order to maintain the vocational center, the classes must have equipment and supplies on a continuous basis. This means that the school deals with hundreds of suppliers and equipment manufacturers.

To accommodate the records of this school, four different filing systems are used. The correspondence and personnel files are alphabetic. (No student files are maintained since they are kept within the student's home school and need not be duplicated at the vocational school.) Requisition files are maintained by subject. That is, the course for which equipment or supplies are needed is the major heading for the subject areas within the requisition files. Administrative files are kept in a subject filing system. By organizing the files in this manner, necessary information can be found easily because it is in a logical order and is set up according to the way in which it is requested.

Procedures Used in Subject Filing

6.3   The basic processes of inspecting, indexing and coding, sorting, and storing remain unchanged in subject filing; hence these are quite similar to those used in alphabetic correspondence filing.

In subject filing, many records deal with more than one subject and may be requested under any one of them. The record itself should be filed under the most important subject and cross-referenced under the other subjects. The illustration on page 74 shows that a letter from *Ralston's Cooking School* was stored in the *Cookware—Misc.* folder because the most important topic of the letter was cookware. However, a cross-reference sheet was stored in the *Administration—Misc.* folder because the letter may be requested by someone on the administrative staff of The Butler's Pantry Equipment Company who needs the information in the last paragraph.

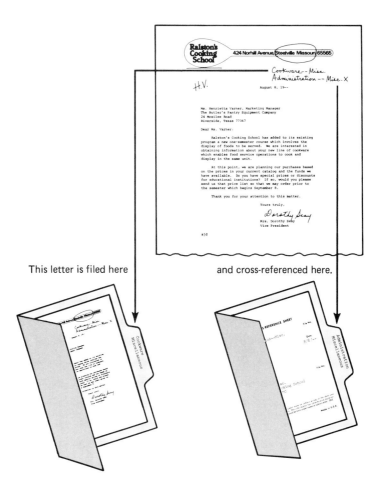

This letter is filed here   and cross-referenced here.

Steps in Subject Correspondence Filing

6.3   **1. Inspecting.** Correspondence is checked to make sure it has been released for filing.

2. Indexing and coding. In a subject-alphabetic system, it is usually necessary to write the subject classification in the upper right-hand corner.

In order to assign a subject caption to correspondence, it is necessary to think about the correspondence. Obviously, if the caption itself appears in the correspondence, the process is easy. If the caption does not appear in the correspondence, you might look for a synonym (a word or phrase that means the same thing as the caption). The most important thing to remember is that other people use the files; it is therefore necessary to assign a caption to the correspondence and file it where it will most often be looked for. You might also find it necessary to cross-reference the correspondence under another caption by which the material might be requested.

3. Sorting. The coded records are sorted into piles first by the main headings. Then these piles are further sorted according to the division of the main heading and then by subdivisions.

4. Storing. The records for each folder are arranged chronologically with the latest date in front.

Kinds of Subject Files

6.4 There are three basic kinds of subject files: (1) *combination,* (2) *alphabetic,* and (3) *numeric.*

STEPS IN THE SUBJECT FILING OF CORRESPONDENCE

1. INSPECTING. Correspondence is checked to make sure it has been released for filing.

2. INDEXING AND CODING. In a subject-alphabetic system it is usually necessary to write the subject classification in the upper right corner. (In the subject-numeric system, the records are coded by writing the folder number in the upper right corner.)

3. SORTING. The coded records are sorted into piles by main headings, whether they are alphabetic or numeric.

Next, these piles are sorted according to the divisions of the main heading; finally, they are sorted by subdivisions.

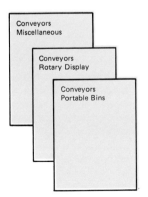

4. STORING. Records for each folder are arranged chronologically with the latest date in front and stored in file drawers.

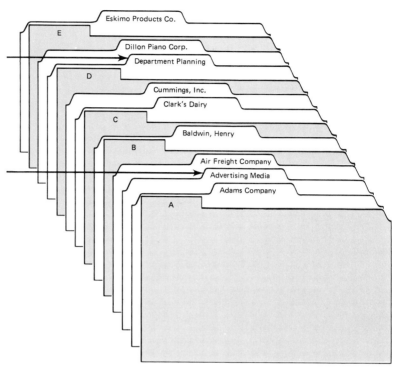

Combination subject file containing subject captions (indicated by arrows) in addition to regular name captions.

6.4   The *combination subject file* illustrated above is used when the volume of correspondence to be grouped by subject is small in comparison with records to be filed under the name of persons or organizations. In this case, the subject captions are combined with the name captions in one file. The folder for *Advertising Media* is stored between folders for *Adams Company* and *Air Freight Company*.

     The *alphabetic subject file*, as the name implies, has subject headings and divisions that are alphabetized. The subject file of the Arena Sporting Mart holds information about the 1,000 sporting goods items that are sold in the store. It contains the following kinds of information: (1) correspondence pertaining to sporting goods items; (2) announcements of new products; (3) brochures and pamphlets describing sporting goods; (4) sales records of each item for past years; (5) price lists and quotations; and (6) miscellaneous records pertaining to specific items. The file is based on the six departments in the store; hence the main subject headings in the file are: *Angling, Camping and Hunting, Games and Toys, Indoor Athletics, Outdoor Athletics,* and *Water Sports.*

In order to make the subject file easier to use, however, an index to the file is needed. For example, let us say that an inexperienced worker is asked to find information in the files about *Archery*. Since archery might be classified under either *Outdoor Athletics* or *Camping and Hunting,* the file worker may not know where to locate the information. A card index (or alphabetic listing) of all headings, divisions, and subdivisions in the file would tell the file worker exactly where to find information on archery. This is called a *relative index*. A section of it can be seen here:

Accessories–Archery –Outdoor Athletics
Accessories–Baseball–Outdoor Athletics
Accessories–Cycling –Outdoor Athletics
Accessories–Football –Outdoor Athletics
Accessories–Golf   –Outdoor Athletics
Archery   –Outdoor Athletics
Arrows–Archery   –Outdoor Athletics
Bags–Golf   –Outdoor Athletics
and so on

The worker would then scan the list (or card index) and find *Archery;* this, in turn, indicates that the file worker should look under the major heading *Outdoor Athletics.*

Outdoor Athletics

ARCHERY
  Accessories
  Arrows
  Bows
  Targets
BASEBALL
  Accessories
  Baseballs
    Hardball
    Softball
  Bats
  Gloves
    Catcher
    Fielder
    First Base
  Protective Equipment
  Uniforms
    Caps
    Shoes
    Suits

CYCLING
  Accessories
  Bicycles
    Ladies and Girls
    Men and Boys
  Children's Cycles
  Motored Equipment
FOOTBALL
  Accessories
  Footballs
  Practice Equipment
  Uniforms
    Helmets
    Padding Equipment
    Shoes
    Suits

Large organizations require subject files with the main categories divided and subdivided. This breakdown of categories is called an *encyclopedic arrangement*. Such an arrangement is illustrated on page 78. In smaller businesses, and where division of topics is not needed, a simpler arrangement like the one shown on page 78 is used. This kind of subject classification is called a *dictionary arrangement*.

ALPHABETIC SUBJECT FILE WITH ENCYCLOPEDIC ARRANGEMENT

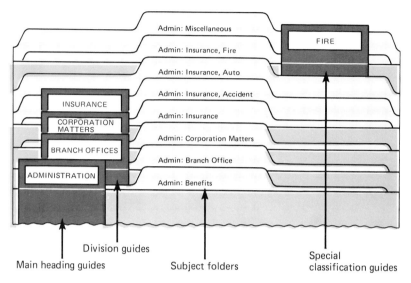

Main heading guides   Division guides   Subject folders   Special classification guides

ALPHABETIC SUBJECT FILE WITH DICTIONARY ARRANGEMENT

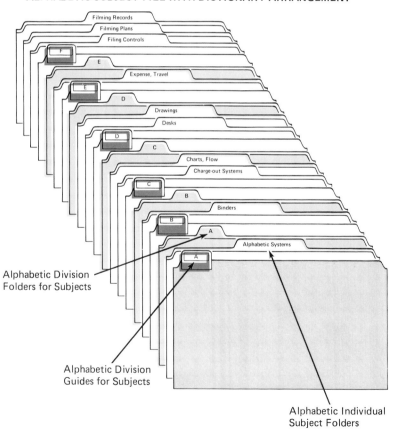

Alphabetic Division Folders for Subjects

Alphabetic Division Guides for Subjects

Alphabetic Individual Subject Folders

6.4   The *numeric subject file,* the third basic kind of subject file, includes several systems that use numbers for captions in place of words. Numbers make coding easier, since it is easier to write numbers on correspondence than subject titles (some subject titles can be very long!). Numeric subject systems can also be expanded easily because new subjects can be assigned a number and placed at the end of the present list of subjects, regardless of their alphabetic arrangement.

In addition, numeric subject systems permit closely related topics to be grouped together in the files. In alphabetic subject files, these topics could easily be filed far apart from each other.

Simple-numeric subject systems are organized by first assigning numbers to the main subject headings in the file. The numbers do not have to be assigned consecutively to the subject headings in an alphabetized list. The list may be organized so that the related topics are together.

These days grocery store chains sell more than food. A grocery chain may organize its files in this way:

Bakery	100
Groceries	200
Meats	300
Produce	400
Sundries	500

Then divisions under each main heading, such as 500 (Sundries), are assigned numbers:

Sundries	500	
Cosmetics		510
Eye-Care Products		520
Games		530
Hair Care Products		540
Laxatives		550

Finally, the subdivisions under each division, such as 550 (Laxatives), would be assigned numbers:

Laxatives	550	
Liquids		551
Tablets		552

After the numbers have been assigned, they are placed on the appropriate guides and folders in the file. In some numeric subject files, the subject as well as the number appears on guides and folders to provide a double check for filing and finding. A card index must also be prepared for a simple-numeric subject file. This index is arranged in the same manner as the relative index discussed earlier, except that each subject refers to a number.

6.4   *Decimal-numeric* subject systems are used when main headings are subdivided more than twice. Let us see how this system would be used to classify *Laxatives*. The same numbers would be assigned as under the simple-numeric system:

Laxatives	550	
Liquids	551	
Children's Strength		551.1
Adult Strength		551.2
Tablets	552	

Adding more digits to the right of the decimal point makes it possible to continue the subdivisions indefinitely. For example, 551.1 could be further subdivided into 551.11, 551.12, 551.13, and so on. This system also requires a card index.

Duplex-numeric subject systems are used when there are more than ten main headings or more than nine divisions or subdivisions under the same heading. For example, suppose the 500 division (Sundries) in the grocery chain file had 11 subdivisions. The following listing illustrates how the duplex-numeric system would provide a number for each of the subdivisions, whereas a simple-numeric or decimal-numeric system would allow for only nine subdivisions.

Subject	Simple-numeric or decimal-numeric	Duplex-numeric
Sundries	500	5
Cosmetics	510	5-1
Eye-Care Products	520	5-2
Games	530	5-3
Hair-Care Products	540	5-4
Laxatives	550	5-5
Liniments	560	5-6
Pain Relievers	570	5-7
Plants	580	5-8
Toys	590	5-9
Vitamins	no provision	5-10
Yarn	no provision	5-11

Further subdivisions are possible with the duplex-numeric system by adding a hyphen and beginning a new series of numbers. Some duplex-numeric systems use a combination of numbers and letters of the alphabet, such as *7, 7-1, 7-2, 7-3, 7-4, 7-4A,* and so on.

Controlling Records

6.6 The major goal of any filing system is *retrieval,* or the quick finding of the records when they are needed. Current records are used more often than records from the last quarter (three months) or the quarter before that. For this reason, some controls need to be placed on the records that are kept in the active files. Just as there are procedures for charging out records, there must also be procedures for transferring records to inactive status.

Transferring Records

Very often, office space is limited, and only so much space can be used for storing records in file cabinets. Records that are used frequently should be stored in easily accessible file cabinets. Such records or files are called *active files*. Because this valuable space fills up, some provision must be made to transfer lesser-used records to *inactive files*. Records that are no longer needed should be destroyed. This procedure saves a great deal of money for any organization in three ways: (1) it reduces the amount of space needed for the active files; (2) it makes possible the use of inexpensive equipment and supplies for the inactive files; and (3) it streamlines the active files so that materials can be filed with utmost efficiency.

When establishing the policy concerning how long filed records are to be kept, careful consideration should be given to the nature of the business, the type of records handled, the information derived from them, and the law. In any such analysis, the following four categories of records are revealed:

1. Vital records. These are essential to the existence of the business and are irreplaceable if destroyed. They should never be transferred.

2. Important records. These facilitate the routine of the business and are replaceable at great cost and much delay. They may be transferred if inactive and placed in cabinets that will keep them in good condition.

3. Useful records. These are temporarily helpful and are replaceable at slight cost. They are often destroyed after three or four years.

4. Nonessential papers. These can be destroyed after temporary use.

Transfer Plans

6.7 Several plans for transfer are available to businesses. The selection of a plan should be based on the nature and frequency of reference, the space available, and the filing system in use. The two general methods are *periodic* and *perpetual*. Each method may be adapted to meet specific situations. Whenever possible, the arrangement of folders in the transfer equipment should correspond to that used in the current files in order to facilitate the finding of material.

Periodic Transfer

Periodic transfer is the removal of records at *stated intervals* (once or twice a year, or at other definite times) from the current, active files to

6.7 the inactive, transfer equipment. Periodic transfer may be operated in one of three ways: one period, two period, or maximum-minimum period.

In the *one-period plan,* only the records for the current filing period occupy the entire capacity of the active files. *All* the folders and their contents of the current period are moved directly from the active files to the inactive files at stated intervals. As soon as this is done, a new filing period begins. The guides usually remain in the active files. The transferred miscellaneous folders are placed in front of the alphabetic subdivision they govern to serve as guides in the inactive files, thereby eliminating the need for two sets of expensive guides.

New individual and miscellaneous folders are prepared for the active files. This transfer plan is a simple one, but it has a definite disadvantage. For a while, frequent trips will have to be made to the transfer files to consult still-active records. If the transfer files are located outside the main office area, such as in a storage room or other such area, much valuable time will be lost.

In the *two-period plan,* the active files are divided to provide space for two classes of material—the current records and those from the last filing period. At the end of each filing period (three months, six months, a year, or whatever length of time was selected between transfer times), all folders and their contents from the *oldest* filing period are moved to the transfer files. The two-period plan requires two sets of active guides and folders—one for the current filing period and one for the last filing period—but it does eliminate the disadvantage of the one-period plan. Because only the older records have been transferred, the current ones and those from the previous period are still readily available in the active files. The illustration on page 83 shows how file drawers may be arranged under a two-period plan to make the most accessible space available for the frequently used papers. Such arrangements will eliminate the fatigue that comes from working in a stooped-over or tip-toe position. *Double capacity, multiple transfer,* and *cycle method* are other terms used to describe the two-period plan.

In the *maximum-minimum period plan,* records are moved directly from the active files to the transfer files. However, the disadvantage of the one-period plan is overcome by keeping some of the recent records in the current file. In this plan, the maximum and minimum periods must be established according to the needs of the business.

For example, suppose the nature of the organization makes it wise for at least a year's correspondence to be kept in the current folders, and the volume of records filed makes transfer necessary every six months. Under the maximum-minimum plan, the minimum would be one year and the maximum 18 months. On January 1, 1982, therefore, there would be in the current files papers going back for a period of 18 months—or to July 1, 1980. The July, 1980, through December, 1980, papers would be removed, leaving on hand for reference purposes the papers of January, 1981, through December, 1981, or the records for one year. At transfer time six months later, or on July 1, 1982, there would again be an accumulation of 18 months' records in the current files. The records for the oldest six-month period—from January, 1981, through June, 1981—would be transferred. The records being transferred can be placed with previously transferred records, or stored in the transfer files by periods.

Under the *perpetual transfer plan,* records are being transferred from the current to inactive files all the time. This plan is generally used when the nature of an organization makes it difficult to set definite periods for transfer. For example, in the type of work done by contractors, architects, or lawyers, or others involved with time periods, the length of time taken to complete the work varies with each job or case. Transferring records on a definite time basis might result in the

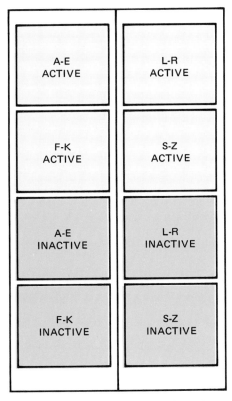

With the two-period plan and four-drawer files, the two upper drawers hold active records and the two drawers below hold inactive records.

6.7 removal of active records. Whenever a specific job or case is completed, all records pertaining to it are moved to the inactive files.

Planning Transfer

The steps illustrated below can be followed *before* the time of actual transfer. By doing so, the file worker will lighten the burden at transfer time. Interference with regular use of the files will also be reduced.

The transfer of records is also discussed in Chapter 10 in regard to micrographics.

STEPS IN PLANNING TRANSFER

1. Prepare a list of correspondents that will need new folders.

2. Type labels for the new folders; prepare the folders.

3. Assemble transfer boxes and label them.

4. Discard previously transferred records that are no longer needed. Authority to discard should be in writing.

◆ HAVE YOU MET YOUR COMPETENCIES?

6.1 Give two examples in which subject correspondence filing would be used in business.

6.2 Arrange these subject captions in order for a subject correspondence file.

Insurance	Accident Insurance
Accounts Receivable	Fire Insurance
Liability Insurance	Accounts Payable
Automobile Insurance	Philadelphia Branch
Accounting	Branch Offices
Tuscaloosa Branch	Norfolk Branch

6.3 List and describe the steps to be followed in subject correspondence filing.

6.4 Describe the three kinds of subject files.

6.5 Assign one of the subject captions below to each statement following the index.

1. Accounting		**14.**	Radio
2.	Expenses	**15.**	TV
3.	Operating	**16.**	Education
4.	Sales	**17.**	Customer Courses
5.	Payroll	**18.**	Employee Training
6. Administration		**19.**	Sales Training
7.	Budget	**20.**	Personnel
8.	Planning	**21.**	Applications
9.	Policies	**22.**	Employment Tests
10.	Research	**23.** Sales	
11. Advertising		**24.**	Retail
12.	Magazines	**25.**	Wholesale
13.	Newspapers		

(1) A salesperson's expense report for the month.

(2) The current budget submitted to the Board of Directors.

(3) A list of prices for wholesale.

(4) Report of the committee researching changes in sales techniques.

(5) Lane Williams' application for the secretarial position open.

(6) Copy for ad in the local daily paper.

(7) Change in policy reported by the Board of Directors.

(8) Lane Williams' employment test results.

(9) A suggested course outline for the training of sales personnel.

(10) A five-year plan for administrative action.

(11) Payroll report for the month.
(12) The retail sales report for the quarter.
(13) A training plan for the secretarial staff.
(14) A script for a commercial on radio station WBPO.
(15) Operating expenses listed by department for the quarter.

6.6 State the advantages of a planned transfer and retention procedure.

6.7 State two or more methods used in transferring documents from active to inactive status.

6.8
TO 6.10 If you have the *Progressive Filing Practice Set,* turn to your *Practice Instruction Manual* and complete Jobs 32 through 39. (Jobs 32 through 34 will enable you to meet Competency 6.7, Job 35 will enable you to meet Competency 6.8, and Jobs 36 through 39 will enable you to meet Competency 6.9.)

Note: If you are using the *Progressive Filing Practice Set,* you should complete Job 40 (Quiz on Subject Filing) before continuing to Chapter 7.

Chapter

7

Organizing Your Work Station

Competencies

7.1 Given examples of items to be filed, indicate whether they should be filed in the "in," "out," or "hold" basket.

7.2 List five or more items that may be kept in a desk-drawer file.

7.3 Given the titles of ten forms, arrange the titles in order so that they can be used as captions for a forms file.

7.4 Given a list of documents to be logged in, prepare a sample log book page for them.

7.5 State the purpose and use of correspondence books.

7.6 Draw a sketch of a desk top and indicate the placement of materials on the desk.

7.7 Given a list of supplies, describe an efficient system for organizing them.

7.8 Name three or more desk-top references.

7.9 Given a list of paperwork, state in what order each item would be handled, and describe what action would be taken.

7.10 Describe two methods of setting up chronological or tickler files.

7.11 Given a case situation in which a new set of papers is to be filed, list procedures for setting up files.

7.12 Given a miniature chronological or tickler report form, record information properly on the form. (See Job 41 in the *Progressive Filing Practice Set.*)

Efficiency experts will tell you that planning tasks take 50 percent of the time involved in performing the whole job. Part of the planning involves general organization. The organization of your desk and work station could easily be your key to success on the job.

"In," "Out," and "Hold"

7.1 The more organized you are, the more apt you are to handle your work efficiently. Many office workers have "in," "out," and "hold" baskets on their desks in which they keep paperwork to be handled, filed, or maintained for action at some later date.

These baskets are actually wooden or metal boxes with no top. Some are stacked with the use of metal braces, which leaves enough room for ease in placing papers into or removing papers from the baskets. Others are simply three boxes placed side by side on the desk. They are generally placed on the right back corner of the desk top. These baskets will allow you to manage your work neatly and efficiently while you deal with the many different tasks your job entails. For example, you might come to work one morning and find the following items in your "in" basket: (1) an expense account form that your employer has filled out in order to be reimbursed (paid back) for a business trip taken the week before; (2) a memo from a person within the company regarding a matter your employer needs to attend to before the day is over; and (3) a routine letter from a customer requesting information from your employer. How would you handle these items?

You would probably place the memo on your employer's desk for immediate attention. You would check the expense account form for accuracy and place it in your "out" basket to be sent to the accounting department. To save time and effort, you would also place the letter from the customer on your employer's desk at the same time you placed the memo there; however, the memo would be on top.

Any items that are to be acted on in the future should be placed in your "hold" basket. The "hold" basket should be checked often to make sure that all items are handled when they need to be.

The Desk-Drawer File

7.2 The desk-drawer file can save much time and energy in your workday. Rarely do two people use a desk-drawer file in the same way. The desk-drawer file can be organized to fit your specific needs. Some office workers find it helpful to keep a supply of frequently used forms in the desk drawer so that they are handy when needed. A "work-in-progress" file is often kept in the drawer so that you can place your work in it at the end of the day; you can keep your work here until you need it. Copies of form letters that need to go out regularly may also be kept in this drawer. A long-range project may require you to do research and to collect information over an extended period of time before you begin working on the project. This material could easily be stored in a file folder in the desk-drawer file.

A number of office workers find that keeping blank file folders in this drawer saves steps to the supply cabinet. Correspondence books, log books, a company policy handbook, a relative index to the files, and any temporary files could also be kept in the desk-drawer file. Letterheads, carbon paper, and second sheets are generally kept in the top right desk drawer; this drawer usually contains sloping sections. However, if your desk is not equipped in this way, you might find the desk-drawer file a good place to keep such supplies.

You will find that the desk file drawer can save you unnecessary steps each day. You will be able to organize the drawer so that it suits your needs. Often, the back of the drawer is a convenient place for you to keep tissues, aspirin, and other personal items so that they will be handy, yet out of the way, when you need them.

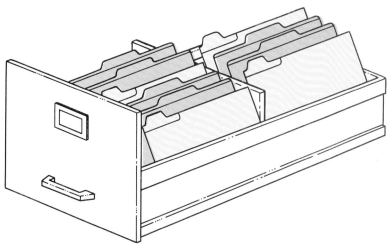

Guides and folders may be stored sideways in a desk-drawer file.

Forms File

7.3   Most businesses use a variety of forms. Your school is a good example. Think of the forms your teacher uses. Attendance forms, enrollment forms, locker assignment sheets, book-room request forms, requisition forms for supplies and equipment, conduct-report forms, suspension notices, interim-report forms, admission slips, corridor passes, field trip request forms, and so on, are all a part of the school's forms file.

In order for your school's office staff to be able to issue these forms when they are needed, a forms file must be maintained. This file could be kept in a file cabinet with folders for each type of form. Sometimes,

7.3 shelves are used to store forms. Each section of the shelf would be labeled and the forms would rest above the label on the shelf. The forms are probably best filed alphabetically according to the name on the form. Some people file forms by number. For example, a conduct report form might have a number such as this: *Form No. 4783-80.* The form number probably indicates something to the people who use it. The number *80* at the end of the form number may indicate the year it was last printed or the year it was last revised. The number *4783* could indicate something to the printer of the form. Perhaps the *4* means that it is printed on four colors of carbonless paper; the *7* might indicate the number of copies in thousands, in this case, 7,000. The *83* may indicate that the form is the eighty-third one the organization has designed.

Some people choose to file forms according to the area of need; for instance, administrative forms and pupil personnel forms would be filed accordingly.

Log Books

7.4 As you have seen, business records are many and varied. Letters, memos, reports, speeches, and financial records are generally one or more pages long and are stored in file folders in cabinets or desk drawers.

A log book, on the other hand, is a different kind of record that is in constant use and is equally important to business operations. Log books are used for a number of purposes. Some are used to record incoming and outgoing phone calls, particularly long distance ones. Others are used to record various types of incoming and outgoing mail. For example, a registered letter, either incoming or outgoing, could be entered in a log book. The log entry may later be used to identify a particular business transaction.

Lawsuits are often won or lost because of the existence of records contained in a log book. A page from a log book is illustrated below (the left half of the page) and on page 91 (the right half of the page).

SPECIAL MAIL LOG				From	
Date	Time of Arrival	Via	Description	Name	Address
July 11	9:20a.m.	PO	Registered letter	Butler's Pantry	Riverside, TX
July 11	3:15p.m.	PO	Insured package	Table Kettle Kitchenware	Springhill, LA
July 11	3:15p.m.	PO	Special Delivery Letter	Van de Meer & Moats	Riverside, TX
July 12	10:50a.m	UPS	3 large parcels	Seafood Cookware	Riverton, KS

Chapter 7. Organizing Your Work Station

Correspondence Books

7.5 As an office worker, one of the most helpful items you can utilize is a correspondence book. Correspondence books are something you make yourself and keep in a loose-leaf binder. You simply prepare an extra copy of correspondence and place it in chronological order within the binder with the most recent item at the front of the book. Correspondence books are used in a number of ways.

Many office workers keep a correspondence book for current correspondence. This is particularly important if you are in an organization with a centralized filing department. A great deal of time can be saved when referring to a letter that went out, say, last Friday. If a copy of the letter were in your correspondence book, you would not have to go to the central filing department to request it. Some people keep all correspondence in the book for a month. Others maintain correspondence for the quarter (three months). Others remove only that correspondence for which business transactions have been completed.

Often, when an office worker has a number of employers for whom correspondence is prepared, a correspondence book becomes an easy reference for finding the letter style preferred by one employer or another.

The Items on Your Desk

7.6 A neatly kept desk is an indication of an organized person. Often, the first impression a caller has of a company or firm is the condition of the first desk the caller approaches. That desk may be yours. It is also important that your desk top be arranged for your own efficiency. Small items such as rubber bands, paper clips, pens and pencils, scissors, erasers, and ruler should be off the desk top and kept in the center drawer of your desk. They are handy there and eliminate a lot of unnecessary clutter on your desk. Some office workers who use such items frequently purchase a rotary-type tray or other decorative desktop container for such items.

To		Delivered			Comments
Name	Department	To	By	Time	
L.E. Turner	Sales	LET	MK	10:05 a.m.	Return receipt signed
D. Castelli	Shipping	DC	messenger	3:25 p.m.	Postage due 72 ¢
I.M. Richter	Legal	IMR	MK	3:30 p.m.	
F. Conroe	Advertising	FC	messenger	11:15 a.m.	One parcel arrived opened

7.6   As was mentioned earlier, the "in," "out," and "hold" baskets are placed on the far right corner of the desk. Often, reference books that are used regularly are placed in a small stand beside these baskets. Such books as the company telephone directory, a reference manual for office workers, a ZIP Code directory, a dictionary, a word-division guide, or other reference books are placed here for easy access.

      Most office workers who use a typewriter have L-shaped desks. The typewriter is placed on the L-return. Often, a calculator is needed for the tasks to be done; if so, a U-shaped desk with two returns would be used so that the calculator could be positioned on the other return. Transcription equipment is generally placed close to the typewriter.

      Other items often needed by office workers include a telephone, a card file for names and addresses, a calendar, and a stapler. The telephone should be placed on the left side of your desk if you are a right-handed person. This means that you answer the phone with your left hand, leaving your right hand free to make notes of the call. The stapler and other items should be placed further back on the desk but within reach.

      Office supply stores have a number of items that can make your work easier and more efficient. Once you become familiar with your work, you might want to check such stores to see if some inexpensive item might make your day brighter and easier.

The Organization of Supplies

7.7 A number of supplies must be available to the office worker, and the organization of these supplies has a lot to do with the worker's efficiency. Most office equipment manufacturers equip the desk for efficient use. For example, the top right drawer of the desk is generally equipped with sloping slots for letterheads, letterhead second sheets, letterhead carbon copy sheets, carbon paper, and onionskin for carbon copies. There are usually small sections in the very front of this drawer to keep letterhead envelopes as well as No. 6 envelopes.

      The large file drawer is an excellent place to keep manila envelopes. As was discussed earlier in this chapter, blank file folders could also be kept in this drawer.

      Other drawers on the right side of the desk might have sections in the front for keeping such miscellaneous supplies as correction fluid or tape, stencil correction fluid, and address labels as well as other supplies you find necessary for daily use.

Sources of Information at the Desk

7.8 Most all office workers find that a dictionary, a word-division guide, and a reference manual are the most useful sources of information to keep handy. If your job requires a great deal of composition at the typewriter, you might find a thesaurus, or a dictionary of synonyms and antonyms, to be extremely helpful to you. If your job requires typing a large amount of correspondence going to a variety of places across the country, a ZIP Code directory will be useful. Or perhaps your job requires a lot of phone calls. A telephone directory might be just the reference book you need. Out-of-town telephone directories may be helpful in your work. Many large organizations print telephone directories for the departments in their company. This type of telephone directory might be helpful to you. Postal regulation manuals could assist you in mailing letters and parcels. Specialized reference material is available for almost any field you can name. Some of these special books might merit a space on your desk.

Handling Paperwork

7.9   Your job may require you to use your judgment skills. You may have to decide how to handle different situations when your employer is not available to do so, and you may be given the authority to handle other situations whether your employer is available or not. You will need to exercise common sense and your knowledge of company policies to make the necessary decisions. For this reason, it is important that you become familiar with your company's policies.

Skills in judgment are perhaps the most difficult skills you will have to develop. With time and experience you will further develop these skills. Observe and listen to others; you can learn a great deal by their experiences—and also by their mistakes.

Some of your duties may include forwarding mail to others, changing or canceling appointments, phoning suppliers, writing routine letters, or taking charge of the office when your employer is out of town.

Assume for a moment that your employer has been called out of town on an emergency. No time was available to prepare you for running the office on your own. Let us discuss some of the things that could occur in your employer's absence.

One of your employer's customers calls in regard to an important contract that has been mailed but not yet received. You are not at all familiar with the transaction because it took place between the customer and your employer. Because of the nature of the mail—a contract—you feel certain that this piece of outgoing mail was logged on the date it was mailed. You look in the log book and find that it was logged in four days ago. You then tell the customer that you will check with the post office and will call back after the contract has been located.

It is important to keep a summary of the things that occur while your employer is away. You might keep it in diary form and attach any letters, reports, or other important papers that are received while your employer is away.

7.9   Perhaps a customer calls and wishes to place an order. You could handle the order and attach a copy of it to your summary for your employer.

What would you do, for example, if a member of a professional organization writes and asks if your employer will accept a nomination for an office in the organization? You probably should not accept such a nomination. Respond in writing that you will bring the matter to your employer's attention; record this information in your summary. Attach a copy of your letter to the summary. You could keep your summary in your "hold" basket until you give the summary to your employer.

DATE	TIME	BUSINESS	ACTION
19– 9/26	9 a.m.	Sunset Motel wrote re Model 7564 scale	Ack'd. letter and sent copy to sales rep.
9/27	2:30	D. Seay, Ralston's, called re missing cover	Told her cover was sent air freight
9/27	3:00	Geo. Loeb wrote asking for 500 dishwasher brochures	Asked MG in Advt. to send brochures
10/1	9 a.m.	Ltr. from Ralston's asking for 2 indicators	Ack'd. ltr. & asked whse. to send indicators

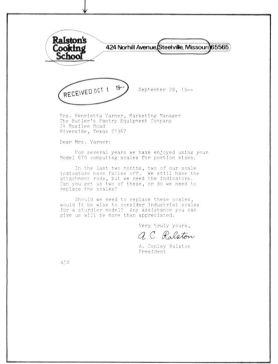

Ralston's Cooking School 424 Norhill Avenue, Steelville, Missouri 65565

RECEIVED OCT 1 19––   September 29, 19––

Mrs. Henrietta Varner, Marketing Manager
The Butler's Pantry Equipment Company
24 Mostlee Road
Riverside, Texas 77367

Dear Mrs. Varner:

     For several years we have enjoyed using your Model 679 computing scales for portion sizes.

     In the last two months, two of our scale indicators have fallen off. We still have the attachment rods, but we need the indicators. Can you get us two of these, or do we need to replace the scales?

     Should we need to replace these scales, would it be wise to consider industrial scales for a sturdier model? Any assistance you can give us will be more than appreciated.

                              Very truly yours,

                              A C Ralston

                              A. Conley Ralston
                              President

ajd

Summaries are used to record phone inquiries and incoming correspondence, such as the letter illustrated here.

It is entirely possible that you would receive correspondence that your employer would want to see before returning. If that is the case, you should have a forwarding address for your employer. In this situation, the original correspondence would be copied and the copies would be sent to your employer. The originals would remain in the "hold" basket until your employer returns.

Any general or routine requests that you would handle ordinarily would continue as usual. But those out-of-the-ordinary office matters that you cannot answer should, if possible, wait until your employer returns. Always have a phone number where you can reach your employer should something urgent arise.

7.10 Tickler (Chronological) Files

It is often very helpful to arrange records by date, or *chronologically*. Most efficient office workers and even some executives use a follow-up file. This is generally called a *tickler file;* other names are *suspense file, pending file, HFA* ("hold for answer") *file,* and *follow-up file.* Whatever the name, this type of file is often the basis for the smooth, punctual flow of work within the office.

In any office, specific things have to be done at specific times. Most people find it unwise to trust everything to memory; therefore, some type of reminder system must be used. The size and needs of the business will determine the best method. However, all *tickler files* are essentially date, or chronological, files.

The simplest of these, and the most familiar, is the *desk calendar* or *calendar pad.* Appointments or activities can simply be listed on the proper page or square for that particular day. The page for any given day gives a quick picture of the day's activities. If many notations have to be made, space limitations make this arrangement impossible. Aside from that, this calendar is "personal" and would not be satisfactory if a number of people had to refer to it for information.

A second kind of tickler file is a *card follow-up system* that can be expanded to handle an unlimited amount of information. The card system consists of 12 month guides, a set of 1 to 31 day guides for the current month, and a desk file such as the one illustrated on page 96. The guides are arranged with the current month guide in the front, followed by the day guides, which are followed by the remaining month guides in sequence. Whenever a matter needs future attention, the name of the person or subject involved, the date, and other necessary information are listed on a 5 × 3 inch card. This card is then stored behind the guide that shows the date the matter must be handled. If it is a matter that will take considerable work, an entry should be made not on the date it must be completed but sufficiently in advance to allow ample time for its completion.

Each morning the reminder cards for that day should be removed from the file. The day guide is then placed behind the guide

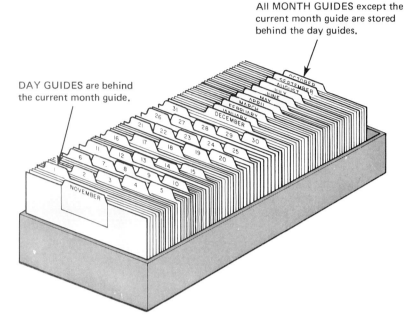

All MONTH GUIDES except the current month guide are stored behind the day guides.

DAY GUIDES are behind the current month guide.

7.10 for the next month; this procedure gets the next month ready for day-by-day division. Next, whatever the cards call for should be done. For example, the first card might indicate that the insurance policy for the company van needs to be renewed. Another might tell you that a price quotation is due from the McDermott Shipping Company; it is then your job to check whether that quotation has arrived and inform your employer. Another card could specify that the Stephens Corporation invoice must be paid today in order to qualify for a discount.

Combining the Date File With an Alphabetic File

In some offices, combining your date, or chronological, file with an alphabetic file might be very helpful. This kind of file works best in small personal files or where some of the pending records have no specific follow-up date. You may use as many alphabetic guides as necessary for this file. Records *with* specific follow-up dates are filed without folders behind the correct day guide. Records *without* specific follow-up dates are filed in individual name or subject folders behind the alphabetic guides.

Follow-Up Folders

Special follow-up folders, like the one illustrated on page 97, are available. These can be used in locating the information needed in follow-up systems. These are date folders that have a straight top edge sheathed in transparent celluloid. The caption is inserted under the celluloid on the left side. Printed under the celluloid to the right of the caption space are the months of the year with the numbers 1 to 31. By sliding a movable pointer to the proper place on the scale, a follow-up date can be indicated. These folders can be kept in a desk-drawer file.

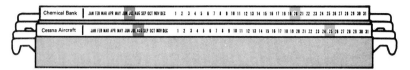

The sliding signals are placed over the month and day that the follow-up is required.

As you can see, most files in offices indicate activities or transactions that have already occurred. However, the follow-up, or tickler, file can be used to organize things that you are planning to do in the future.

Designing a System for Filing

7.11   At some point, you may have the responsibility for designing a file system from "scratch." There is no special way to set up files. Two businesses rarely use the same filing system. There are, however, *guidelines* that you can follow to set up a filing system that can best meet the needs of the people who are going to use the system. The guidelines listed here should be considered for the specific filing needs of the business.

In order to determine what kind of filing system you need, you must:

1. Define the problem. What type of materials will be filed? Should all materials be kept in one filing system, or should more than one system be kept to accommodate the types of records the company uses? Some businesses file correspondence and invoices in the same files because they don't have a large number of each type to file. You may find that your business needs correspondence files as well as another file for invoices or shipping orders.

Should an alphabetic file system be implemented? Should the system be subject, geographic, or numeric? Or should a combination of these be used? If you worked in an insurance firm, you might find that your files could be used easily if you filed correspondence alphabetically and kept another type of file by subject so that you could find information on *term insurance, endowment policies,* and other subjects. A numeric file might also be necessary for filing customers' policies by number.

What are the goals of your filing system? What records must be accessible to whom and in what area of the building? What records are

7.11 necessary but are not used often? Do you need some records more often than others? You might find that, because the receptionist types all the correspondence for your insurance company, the correspondence files should be located near the desk. The customers' policies, however, are used by the insurance agents and need to be positioned close to the agents' work area. Some files may only be used once in a while; these may be placed in a storage area, out of the way but easily accessible when needed. Once you determine the goals of your filing system, it is time to move to step two of the process.

2. Plan your system. After you have determined just what type of system you will use, begin to plan the layout of your filing system. You need to put on paper what type of system you will have, where the files will be located, and who will be using each.

3. Analyze the situation. Once you have the plan on paper, talk with various people who will be using the files to see if they can come up with better ideas and suggestions—or perhaps they can point out problems that may arise.

4. Design your system. Taking into consideration all of the comments and suggestions, revise and update your plan for a system that is clear, easy to use, and easy to change.

Insurance agents, for example, may think the correspondence files should be placed in their work area, or that the policies would best be maintained by the receptionist. Whatever the decision, give it a try.

5. Implement the system. Put the system into practice, informing *all* people who will be using it of its design and of charge-out, transfer, and other procedures. After a reasonable length of time, it will be necessary to check to see if the system works.

6. Evaluate. Plan to check with the people who use this filing system to see if it meets their needs. Ask if the records have been easy to find, easy to return, and easy to locate when checked out. Depending on the answers you receive when you evaluate your system, you may need to revise the system.

You might also be responsible for converting an existing filing system to one that is more efficient. Typical problems that make it necessary to convert a filing system might be too little space, misfiling, records are not properly located for the most efficient use, or perhaps the process necessary to request and return files takes much too long. Your company may need to expand its files and convert to a system that will accommodate the larger number of records. There are steps to use in converting just as there are steps in establishing files. Once again, these are merely guidelines that provide you with a method to make a conversion. No two companies will ever convert from the same system to another similar one.

1. Survey the old system and its users. Ask the users why the old system is no longer functional. Find out what needs to be corrected. Find out what your new goals are and how they differ from the goals of the original filing system.

You may find that you need to rearrange your files so that more people will be able to use them. You may need a new type of charge and transfer procedure so that it is easier to find files that are checked out. Perhaps the agents are not always able to find the files they need because papers have been misfiled.

2. Design a new system to fit your needs. Find out what would make your system meet its new goals. For example, relocation of the files so that enough space is available might solve your problems. Color coding the files might allow for immediate location of misfiled information. Perhaps new equipment or supplies might solve the problems.

3. Work closely with others. People who use the files know best just what the shortcomings are. Find out from them what characteristics the new system should have to better serve the needs of people using the files.

4. Allow for future expansion. Make sure your new system accommodates the future. If you convert your system now, be sure that you will not have to do so again very soon.

5. Plan your new system. Keeping items 3 and 4 in mind, put your system on paper as you did in planning an original system. Remember to check with the people who use the files to see if your new system will be easy for them to use.

Several other problems might arise at this point. A cost analysis might be necessary if you plan to purchase new equipment and supplies. Is it worth the cost to save the time, space, and effort? If so, by all means, do so. Analyze the advantages of your new system. If it is worth the cost, make the changes.

Security is another consideration when designing your filing system. If important records can be easily lost or stolen, the files are *too* accessible. The floor plan of the company needs to be considered, too. If at all possible, records should be kept in areas where they will be needed. Inactive files should be out of the way, but accessible.

6. Train the personnel who will use your system. Make certain that all personnel who will be working with the new system are properly trained. The charge-out and transfer procedures necessary should be firmly fixed in the minds of those who use the files. This will insure proper storage of records and information. It will also do much for the morale of the employees to know they have a workable system that is easy to use.

7. Implement your new system. Put the system into practice once you feel the personnel really know how to use it.

8. Evaluate. Once again, you might wait a reasonable length of time and check to see if the system is working. If not, some rearranging might be necessary. Revising the system to meet the needs of those who use it will ensure its success.

Whatever your system, it should have these three basic characteristics: (1) It should be an adequate system keyed for quick reference and it should be easily accessible to all who need it. (2) It should have a charge-out and transfer procedure that enables file workers to keep track of records that are out of the files. (3) The personnel who use it should know the system and work with it efficiently.

The efficiency of a filing system is most important. Remember, the major goal of *any* filing system is *retrieval*. People who use the files must be able to do so with a minimal amount of effort. The easier it is to use the files, the happier the personnel will be—and the smoother the office will run.

◆ HAVE YOU MET YOUR COMPETENCIES?

7.1 For the items below, indicate in which of the three baskets—"in," "out," or "hold"—each might be found upon your arrival at your desk in the morning.

1. An order to be filled for a customer.
2. A summary sheet for your employer while your employer is out of town.
3. A letter requesting that your employer speak at a banquet next month. Your employer is out of the office for the rest of the day.
4. A request for a file regarding insurance on the company trucks.
5. A request for information from a customer. This letter must be answered by your employer. (Remember, your employer is out of the office for the rest of the day.)
6. Mail to be forwarded to another department within your company. (You took care of this matter yesterday.)
7. A letter that requires a response from your employer. (Remember where your employer is!)

7.2 List five or more items that might be kept in a desk-drawer file.

7.3 Arrange the following form titles in order so that they can be used as the captions for a forms file.

1. Appraisal Forms
2. Listing Contracts
3. Cash Receipts Forms
4. Closing Cost Forms
5. Deed of Sale Forms
6. Sales Contracts

7. Competitive Analysis Forms

8. Estimate Forms

9. Deed of Trust Forms

10. Notification of Closing Costs Forms

7.4 Prepare a sample log book page and then log in the following items:

1. A check enclosed in an envelope marked *registered* from Mr. Ronald Wiggins.
2. Legal records sent via certified mail from Mr. George Owens.
3. Deed of Trust delivered by post office and insured by the sender, Ms. Roberta Milstein.

7.5 State the purpose and use of correspondence books.

7.6 Draw a sketch of a desk top and indicate the placement of the following materials on the desk:

stapler

calculator

"in," "out," and "hold" baskets

address card file

calendar pad

typewriter

resource materials

telephone

7.7 Describe an efficient system for organizing the following supplies on or in your desk:

a book of synonyms

three frequently-used forms

work-in-progress file

stapler

job procedures manual

No. 10 envelopes

address card file

correspondence book

blank file folders

relative index to files

aspirin

letterhead

address labels

postal regulation manual

7.8 Name three or more desk-top references.

7.9 The following is a list of paperwork to be handled. State in what order each item would be handled and describe what action would be taken.

1. A parcel post package received from McDavid & Co., which should have been delivered to the Purchasing Department.
2. A letter changing an appointment your employer has with Mrs. L. A. Stevens from October 12 at 1:30 p.m. to October 13 at 1:00 p.m.

3. An order that was to be delivered to your office yesterday from Kazinski and Stone Office Supply. It has not arrived.

4. An invitation for your employer to attend a banquet in two weeks. It is marked "RSVP by October 13." You know that your employer will be out of town on the day of the banquet.

7.10 Describe two methods of setting up chronological or tickler files.

7.11 Read the following case situation and list the procedures you would follow in setting up files.

You are working in the new office of a chain of drugstores, named Donald Drug Stores, Inc. There are four branches of the store within the region your office will deal with. Paperwork that will be handled and need to be filed will consist of correspondence from customers, manufacturers, and branch offices, as well as reports of various sorts from the branch stores, information regarding new drugs and other products on the market, and prescription forms.

7.12 If you are using the *Progressive Filing Practice Set,* complete Job 41.

Chapter

Numeric
Filing Systems

Competencies

8.1	State two advantages of numeric filing.
8.2	State three business situations in which numeric filing is used.
8.3	Given a series of numbers to be organized for a consecutive numeric system, arrange them in sequence.
8.4	Given a series of numbers to be organized in a terminal-digit file, arrange the numbers in terminal-digit sequence.
8.5	Describe the organization of a numeric correspondence file.
8.6	Given a numeric card file and cards to be filed in a consecutive numeric system, file and find the cards. (See Jobs 42 through 44 in the *Progressive Filing Practice Set.*)
8.7	Given a numeric card file and cards to be filed in a terminal-digit numeric system, file and find the cards. (See Jobs 45 through 48 in the *Progressive Filing Practice Set.*)

Just as names are used in an alphabetic system for file folder and guide captions, *numbers* are used as captions on the guide and folder tabs in *numeric* filing systems. We can say that alphabetic systems are *direct* because a person can go directly to the files and locate or store records. Numeric systems are indirect because, in most cases, before records can be placed in or taken out of the file drawer, the file worker must refer to an alphabetic card index to find the number assigned to a name or subject.

8.1
8.2
 Even though it is indirect, there are numerous advantages to using a numeric system. Consider the following circumstances:

1. Some businesses group their activities around particular cases, contracts, or operations that continue for a relatively long, but indefinite, period of time. These records may require permanent and extensive cross-reference. For example, a lawyer may represent the same client in a number of different cases. By having a separate, numbered folder for each case, records can be located faster than by mixing all the records of the different cases in one folder with the client's name as a caption.
2. Some businesses use numbers as a frame of reference rather than a name. For example, various departments within a business concern themselves with activities that relate primarily to a number and not a person's name. Accounting departments often file vouchers by number; insurance companies use policy numbers rather than the policyholder's name; storerooms and manufacturing departments frequently file and refer to orders by the order number rather than by the names of the customers. It is often quite helpful and efficient to keep confidential records by number and thereby conceal the names of the people involved from workers who handle the files.

Consecutive Numeric System

8.3
 The consecutive numeric system is the most commonly used numeric system. This system, of course, uses consecutive numbers—*1, 2, 3, 4, 5, 6, 7,* and so on. Room numbers within a building are generally consecutive. For example, *room 101* precedes *102,* which precedes *103,* and so forth. Prescription numbers are filed by number in drugstores. *Prescription number 3487* precedes *3488,* which precedes *3489,* and so on.

◆ FILING PRACTICE

8.6 Complete Jobs 42 through 44 in the *Progressive Filing Practice Set,* if you are using it. Otherwise, continue reading.

8.4 Another type of numeric filing is the *terminal-digit system.* The numbers in this system do not just run in sequence as in a consecutive numeric system. Instead, numbers are assigned for a purpose—to classify or group. Such a system is easily learned as long as the basic principles of consecutive numeric filing are understood.

The illustration below compares the consecutive numeric system and the terminal-digit system.

COMPARISON OF CONSECUTIVE NUMERIC AND TERMINAL-DIGIT SYSTEMS

right to left

If you were filing business forms bearing these numbers:

```
23753
23747
23750
23752
23756
23755
```

1. In a consecutive numeric system, they would all be filed in numeric order in one drawer (starred).

2. In a terminal-digit system, the numbers would first be broken into these groups:

Sequence in folder	Folder number	Drawer number
2	37	47
2	37	50
2	37	52
2	37	53
2	37	55
2	37	56

Reading the numbers from right to left, you would then file the forms first by drawer number, then by folder number, and finally by sequence within the folder. Thus the six forms would be stored in six separate file drawers in folder number 37.

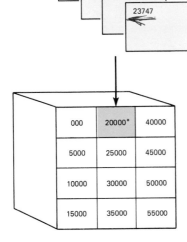

000	20000*	40000
5000	25000	45000
10000	30000	50000
15000	35000	55000

45	49	53*
46	50*	54
47*	51	55*
48	52*	56*

When many forms have to be filed by several file workers, the terminal-digit system is an advantage because it overcomes crowded working conditions by spreading the work over several file drawers.

◆ FILING PRACTICE

8.7   Complete Jobs 45 through 47 in the *Progressive Filing Practice Set,* if you are using it. Otherwise, continue reading.

Organizing a Numeric Correspondence File

8.5   Most numeric correspondence filing systems contain three parts:

1. The main numeric file that contains individual folders bearing numeric captions.
2. A miscellaneous alphabetic file that contains miscellaneous folders bearing alphabetic captions.
3. A card index in which the names of correspondents or subjects are arranged alphabetically. When papers are to be filed or found, this index is consulted to find the numeric caption of the folder.

     In addition to the card index, a register is often kept in which the consecutive numbers that have been—or will be—assigned to folder captions are shown.

NO.	NAME	DATE
818	Hancock, Phillip E.	12/6/--
819	Avco Inc.	12/6/--
820	Young and Stephens Co.	12/7/--
821	G-W Builders Supply	12/10/--
822	Noland Wholesale Inc.	12/14/--
823	Bullock, J. D. Jr.	12/14/--
824	Louise's Shop	12/17/--
825	Johnson-Whitney Furn. Co.	12/17/--
826		
827		
828		

A numeric file register.

Main Numeric File

When records are filed in a numeric system, a number is assigned consecutively to each correspondent or subject that merits an individual folder as these correspondents or subjects develop. Once assigned, a number is maintained until a correspondent no longer does business with the firm, or until a subject ceases to exist. The number may then be reassigned after a specified length of time. All records pertaining to the correspondent or subject are placed in the individual folder bearing the number assigned to that correspondent or subject.

There are different methods of arranging numeric guides in a file drawer. Guides may be staggered in three positions across the file drawer. Guide captions may be numbered in 10s or 20s, whatever interval is most efficient for the firm (this will depend on the number of folders that must be accommodated behind the guides).

The main numeric file contains individual folders. They are arranged in numeric sequence in back of the appropriate guide. As in an alphabetic system, the arrangement of records within the individual folders is chronological, with the latest date in front.

When a folder reaches its capacity, it can then be subdivided by date or subject, according to the way the records will be requested. Subdivided folders generally bear auxiliary numbers to help identify them. For example, folder 1903, after it is subdivided, would become folder 1903-1 and 1903-2. Both would then be arranged in sequence behind folder 1902.

Two other plans for arranging guides and folders in a numeric system are as follows:

1. The guides appear at the left only, in two or three positions. Folders with tabs are then used in the last position on the right.
2. The guides appear in the center only, and folders with tabs are used in two positions—to the right and to the left of the guide.

Miscellaneous Alphabetic File

Until sufficient papers have accumulated for a correspondent or subject, no number or place in the main numeric file is assigned. These papers are filed *alphabetically* in the miscellaneous file. This miscellaneous alphabetic file can be kept in the front part of the first file drawer of the main numeric file, in a separate drawer of the main numeric file, or in an entirely separate file cabinet—whichever is most accessible for the business that uses it.

When enough papers, usually five, have accumulated under one name or subject in the miscellaneous file, the first unused number is assigned to that name or subject. The papers are then placed in a folder of that number and moved to the main numeric file.

As in other systems, unused folders are kept in a convenient place, usually in a file drawer. The file number for a new name is determined by checking the first unused folder. Sometimes a register similar to the one illustrated on page 106 is kept showing the names and numbers assigned.

Card Index

8.5 A card index, which is a list that will identify the assigned numbers, is one of the most important elements of a numeric system. Each card contains the name of a correspondent or subject and the number of the folder that has been assigned. The symbol *M* is used on the cards of correspondents and subjects whose records are stored in the miscellaneous alphabetic file. This *M* is replaced by a permanent number if the correspondent or subject is assigned an individual folder in the main numeric file. All cards in the card index are arranged *alphabetically.*

USING A MISCELLANEOUS ALPHABETIC FILE WITH A NUMERIC FILE

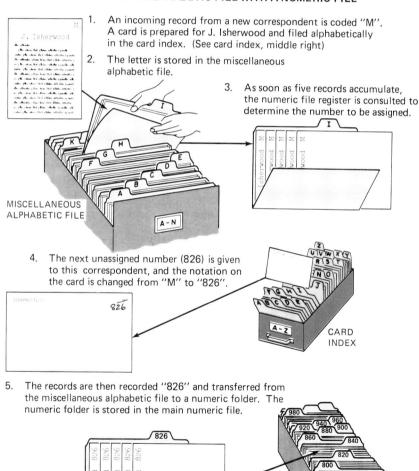

1. An incoming record from a new correspondent is coded "M". A card is prepared for J. Isherwood and filed alphabetically in the card index. (See card index, middle right)

2. The letter is stored in the miscellaneous alphabetic file.

3. As soon as five records accumulate, the numeric file register is consulted to determine the number to be assigned.

MISCELLANEOUS ALPHABETIC FILE

4. The next unassigned number (826) is given to this correspondent, and the notation on the card is changed from "M" to "826".

CARD INDEX

5. The records are then recorded "826" and transferred from the miscellaneous alphabetic file to a numeric folder. The numeric folder is stored in the main numeric file.

Cross-Reference

In alphabetic systems, a cross-reference sheet telling just where the record is stored is placed in all other folders where a person might look for the record. In a numeric system, cross-referencing is done only in the card index. As the illustration below shows, a worker looking for information in the card index about the Mannheim Machines Company would be referred to the Office Machines folder number 697.

```
Mannheim Machines Company
Chicago, Illinois 60611

SEE  Office Machines   697
```

Cross-reference card in the card index to the main
numeric file.

Numeric Filing Procedures

The steps used in numeric filing are quite similar to those used in alphabetic systems.

In numeric coding, if the card index shows that no number has been assigned to a correspondent or subject, an *M* is placed in the upper right-hand corner to indicate that the record is to be stored in the miscellaneous alphabetic file. When five records have accumulated for a correspondent or subject, the records are transferred from the miscellaneous alphabetic file to a numeric file. A number is obtained for it by consulting the numeric file register.

In numeric sorting, the records are arranged first by hundreds, then by tens, and finally into correct numeric sequence. The records coded *M* are placed in one pile during numeric sorting and are then sorted alphabetically.

When storing records coded *M,* each record should be placed in the proper folder in the miscellaneous alphabetic file.

The storing of records that have numeric coding must be done with great care. Reading the coded numbers and the folder numbers to avoid transposition of figures is of the utmost importance. Number 2453, for example, could easily be misread as 2435. Such an error is not likely to be noticed as much as the misspelling of a name. Because such errors are easily made and very difficult to locate, many businesses and organizations with numeric filing systems check them periodically for accuracy.

STEPS IN THE NUMERIC FILING OF CORRESPONDENCE

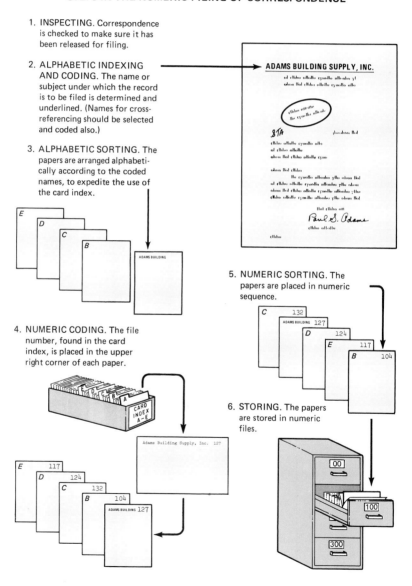

1. INSPECTING. Correspondence is checked to make sure it has been released for filing.

2. ALPHABETIC INDEXING AND CODING. The name or subject under which the record is to be filed is determined and underlined. (Names for cross-referencing should be selected and coded also.)

3. ALPHABETIC SORTING. The papers are arranged alphabetically according to the coded names, to expedite the use of the card index.

4. NUMERIC CODING. The file number, found in the card index, is placed in the upper right corner of each paper.

5. NUMERIC SORTING. The papers are placed in numeric sequence.

6. STORING. The papers are stored in numeric files.

◆ HAVE YOU MET YOUR COMPETENCIES?

8.1 State two advantages of numeric filing.

8.2 State three business situations in which numeric filing is used.

8.3 Arrange the following numbers in correct order for a consecutive numeric filing system.

1734	1619
1819	1743
1745	1739
1602	1691
1835	1929
1878	1887
1601	1688
1833	1871
1693	1877
1834	1831
1931	1919
1621	1816
1727	1618

8.4 Arrange the following numbers in correct order for a terminal-digit filing system. Use the fifth digit (the one at the far right of the number) for the number of the drawer. Use the third and fourth digits for the number of the folder. Finally, use the first and second digits for the sequence in the folder.

10-301	30-312
20-402	30-122
10-107	10-303
10-203	20-319
10-111	30-124
30-121	20-400
10-304	30-315
20-412	10-416
20-418	20-403
10-419	30-126
20-419	20-304
30-314	30-118
10-412	

8.5 Describe the organization of a numeric correspondence file.

8.6   Have you successfully completed Jobs 42 through 47 in the *Progressive*
8.7   *Filing Practice Set?*

Note: If you are using the *Progressive Filing Practice Set,* you should complete Job 48 (Quiz on Numeric Card Filing) before continuing to Chapter 9.

Chapter

Geographic
Filing Systems

Competencies

9.1	State three business situations in which geographic filing is used.
9.2	Describe the captions for guides and folders in a geographic file drawer.
9.3	Explain the use of a card index and a cross-reference sheet in geographic filing.
9.4	Given a list of geographic captions, arrange them in correct order.
9.5	Describe the steps to be followed in geographic correspondence filing.
9.6	Given a geographic card file and cards, file and find the cards. (See Jobs 49 through 51 in the *Progressive Filing Practice Set.*)
9.7	Given a list of geographic captions and miniature correspondence, list the captions under which each item of correspondence is to be filed. (See Jobs 52 through 54 in the *Progressive Filing Practice Set.*)

9.1 Some businesses conduct and control their operations according to districts. Businesses with branch offices often organize their records by regions. Real estate firms, government agencies, and public utilities also may find it advantageous to use a geographic filing system. Such a system is based on the alphabetic arrangement of records first by *location* and then by name or subject.

Three factors must be considered when organizing a geographic filing system: (1) the type of business; (2) the use made of the records; and (3) the geographic locations in which the company has activities. Whatever the specific differences within the system, certain basic features are common to all geographic filing systems.

Arranging the File Drawer

9.2 The names of the largest or most important geographic divisions occurring in the operations of the business generally appear on the primary guides in the file drawer. The secondary guides are used for subdivisions of the main geographic units, as well as for alphabetic sections of the geographic divisions and subdivisions.

In the illustration on page 115, the largest geographic divisions are states. The subdivisions shown are cities or towns in those states. Some businesses might use foreign countries as the main divisions and towns or cities in those countries as the subdivisions. Some organizations use towns or cities as the main divisions and streets as the subdivisions. The filing needs of the business will determine the geographic divisions used.

Folders

9.4 Just as in other systems, an individual folder is started whenever a correspondent justifies one—or has at least five pieces of correspondence to place in the folder. The caption on the folder lists the name of the city or town first, the state second, and then the correspondent. The city or town name is listed first because the city or town guide is nearer to the folder than the state guide. This makes it easier to check to see that records are being filed correctly. Records within the individual folder are filed chronologically, with the latest date on top.

A caption that includes the name of a country and a city would give the name of the country (beginning with the political designation) first and the city second.

Two kinds of miscellaneous folders are used—town or city miscellaneous folders and state miscellaneous folders. Records that pertain to miscellaneous towns in a state are stored in the state miscellaneous folder until enough papers have accumulated to justify opening a miscellaneous folder for that town or city. Records in the city or town miscellaneous folder are arranged alphabetically by the name of the corre-

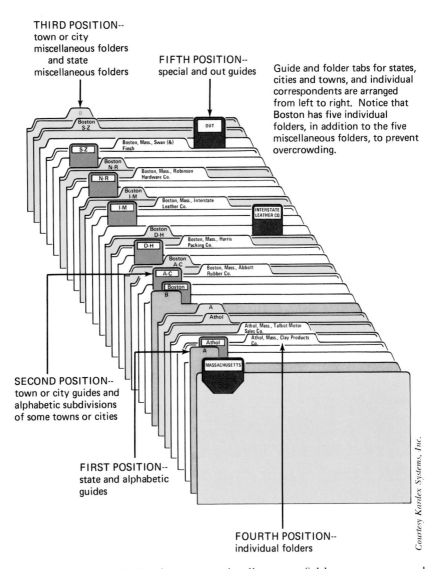

THIRD POSITION--
town or city
miscellaneous folders
and state
miscellaneous folders

FIFTH POSITION--
special and out guides

Guide and folder tabs for states,
cities and towns, and individual
correspondents are arranged
from left to right. Notice that
Boston has five individual
folders, in addition to the five
miscellaneous folders, to prevent
overcrowding.

SECOND POSITION--
town or city guides and
alphabetic subdivisions
of some towns or cities

FIRST POSITION--
state and alphabetic
guides

FOURTH POSITION--
individual folders

Courtesy Kardex Systems, Inc.

spondent. Records in the state miscellaneous folder are arranged alphabetically—first by the name of the town or city and then by the name of the correspondent in the town or city.

Card Index

9.3   A card index is not quite as important in a geographic file as it is in numeric filing systems. However, it can be very helpful to people who cannot remember the geographic location involved. Each card contains the name of a correspondent and the geographic location. The cards are arranged *alphabetically* by names of correspondents.

Cross-Reference

9.3   A cross-reference sheet, such as the one for Portland, Oregon, below, is used if a cross-reference from one location to another occurs in a single record only and is not likely to occur again.

A *permanent* cross-reference from one location to another may be made by using a half-folder with a tab and storing it the same way you would store a folder. The Rollins Metal Plant in Atlanta, Georgia, has a number of subsidiary offices located in different parts of the country. One of these offices is the Metal-Rol Corporation in Pittsburgh, Pennsylvania. In order to keep all this company correspondence together, it is indexed and filed under Atlanta, Georgia. Because this is to be a permanent cross-reference, a Manila half-folder with a cross-reference caption on the tab is prepared.

Geographic cross-reference sheet

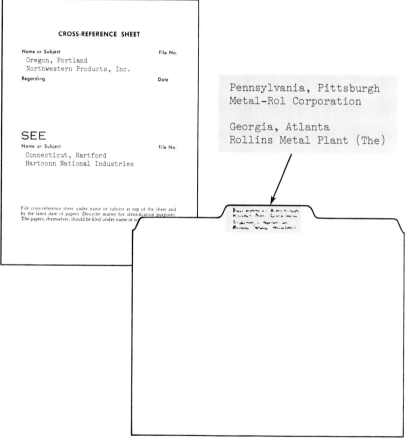

CROSS-REFERENCE SHEET

Name or Subject   File No.
Oregon, Portland
Northwestern Products, Inc.
Regarding   Date

SEE
Name or Subject   File No.
Connecticut, Hartford
Hartconn National Industries

File cross-reference sheet under name or subject at top of the sheet and by the latest date of papers. Describe matter for identification purposes. The papers, themselves, should be filed under name or s[...]

Pennsylvania, Pittsburgh
Metal-Rol Corporation

Georgia, Atlanta
Rollins Metal Plant (The)

Manila tabbed geographic cross-reference half-folder

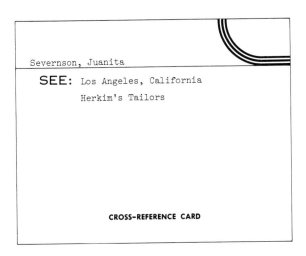

Severnson, Juanita

SEE: Los Angeles, California

Herkim's Tailors

CROSS-REFERENCE CARD

In geographic systems, a cross-reference from an individual to a location is possible only when a card index is used. For example, all correspondence in connection with Herkim's Tailors of Los Angeles, California, is done directly with Ms. Juanita Severnson. Although the correspondence is indexed and filed geographically under *Los Angeles, California, Herkim's Tailors,* it might also be requested under Ms. Severnson's name. For this reason, a card under the name of *Severnson, Juanita,* referring to *Los Angeles, California, Herkim's Tailors,* is filed alphabetically in the card index.

Geographic Filing Procedures

9.5   The steps in geographic filing are quite similar to those used in alphabetic filing.

The correspondence is first *inspected* to see if it has been released for filing. It is then *indexed* and *coded.* The name of the correspondent and the location under which the record is to be filed are both determined. Some file workers underline the name and circle the location. Names for cross-referencing should also be selected and coded at this time.

Sorting requires two steps. The records are first sorted by main geographic division; then these main units are sorted into geographic subdivisions.

The final step, of course, is *storing.* The state and city or town guides are used to locate the proper folder section rapidly. The appropriate alphabetic part of the folder section is then scanned for an individual folder for the coded name. If there is none, the record is placed in a miscellaneous folder.

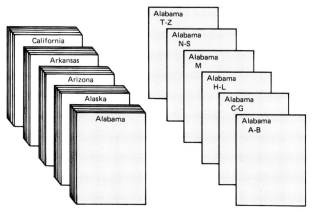

Records are sorted first by main geographic division. Next, these main units are sorted into geographic subdivisions.

◆ HAVE YOU MET YOUR COMPETENCIES?

9.1 State three business situations in which geographic filing is used.

9.2 Describe the captions for guides and folders in a geographic file drawer.

9.3 Explain the use of a card index and a cross-reference sheet in geographic filing.

9.4 Arrange the following geographic captions in correct order.

Type or write the following states and cities on 5 × 3 inch cards. Place the number that appears beside each in the upper right-hand corner of the card. After you have typed (or written) the cards, arrange them in order for a geographic file.

1. Charleston, West Virginia
2. Parkersburg, West Virginia
3. Fairmont, West Virginia
4. Bridgeport, West Virginia
5. Pierre, South Dakota
6. Sioux Falls, South Dakota
7. Harrisburg, Pennsylvania
8. Pittsburgh, Pennsylvania
9. Philadelphia, Pennsylvania
10. Nashville, Tennessee
11. Memphis, Tennessee
12. Knoxville, Tennessee
13. Sweetwater, Tennessee
14. New Orleans, Louisiana

15. Baton Rouge, Louisiana
16. Hammond, Louisiana
17. Jackson, Mississippi
18. Biloxi, Mississippi
19. Boston, Massachusetts
20. Hyannis Port, Massachusetts
21. New Bedford, Massachusetts
22. Chicago, Illinois
23. Joliet, Illinois
24. Decatur, Illinois
25. Springfield, Illinois

As in the exercise above, type or write the following countries and cities on 5 × 3 inch cards. Place the number that appears beside each in the upper right-hand corner of the card. After you have typed (or written) the cards, arrange them in order for a geographic file.

1. Republic of Bolivia, La Paz
2. Republic of Bolivia, Sucre
3. Republic of Bolivia, Santa Cruz
4. Kingdom of Afghanistan, Kabul
5. Kingdom of Afghanistan, Herat
6. Union of Burma, Rangoon
7. Union of Burma, Mandalay
8. Republic of Cuba, Guantánamo
9. Republic of Cuba, Havana
10. Republic of Cuba, Santa Clara
11. Kingdom of Denmark, Copenhagen
12. Kingdom of Denmark, Randers
13. Kingdom of Laos, Vientiane
14. Republic of Finland, Helsinki
15. Republic of Finland, Turku
16. Republic of Finland, Tampere
17. State of Israel, Jerusalem
18. State of Israel, Tel Aviv
19. State of Israel, Jaffa
20. State of Israel, Haifa
21. Republic of Tunisia, Tunis
22. Republic of Tunisia, Gafsa
23. Dominion of New Zealand, Wellington
24. Dominion of New Zealand, Dunedin
25. Dominion of New Zealand, Auckland

After you have arranged the cards for a geographic file, list the numbers in the order they now appear on an answer sheet. Turn in your answer sheet to your teacher for checking.

9.5 Describe the steps in geographic correspondence filing.

9.6 Have you successfully completed Jobs 49 through 53 in the *Progressive*
9.7 *Filing Practice Set?*

Note: If you are using the *Progressive Filing Practice Set,* complete Job 54
(Quiz on Geographic Filing) before continuing to Chapter 10.

Chapter

10

File Systems for Modern Office Technology

Competencies

10.1   Given a list of items to be logged in for word processing equipment, prepare a log book page and record the documents in the log book.

10.2   Given a list of ten types of business records, select those that are likely to be filmed.

10.3   State the advantages of commercial systems in filing.

The continuing use of computers, automatic typewriters and typeset-ting equipment for word processing, and various micrographics facili-ties has made it necessary for businesses to handle and file records that differ in size and format (as well as use) from paper records. Manufac-turers have had to provide filing equipment to go with the various types of office machines they sell.

Word Processing

A good example of this is the ever-increasing use of word processing equipment. These machines may use large or small tape cartridges, magnetic cards, paper tape, or floppy disks. These kinds of media must be made a part of either temporary or permanent records for busi-nesses and organizations that use word processing equipment. For that reason, they must be filed or stored in such a way that they can be lo-cated easily when they are needed. It is often necessary for that same container to hold a copy of the material that is recorded on the media. If no copy is necessary, instructions for the use of the particular media must be available to the person who uses them.

One company that sells a magnetic card typewriter has developed a small folder into which the card is easily inserted. Each card is num-bered by the company that sells the cards. There is a place on the folder for the card number; there is also room to record a title or description of what is on the card, as well as instructions for its use. These instruc-tions might include nothing more than the margin and tab settings on the typewriter, or they might include lengthy information about what to do when the typewriter stops, or what line the material needs to begin on. They might even state that the material contained on the card is confidential.

Some manufacturers have included with the automatic typewriters a desk onto which the typewriter is permanently fixed. One or more of the drawers in that desk are equipped to hold tape cartridges neatly in place. Other manufacturers have developed revolving stands in which specified numbers of tapes can be stored. The tapes are labeled with numbers or titles of projects and the label extends from within the stand. Hence people who use these tapes can easily see which tape or tapes they need.

Word Processing Logs

10.1   Because it is necessary to know what to do with these kinds of media, and because they are not usable in their stored form, a log is necessary. These logs range from simple to complex.

Many large organizations have word processing departments which serve a large number of people in other departments or divisions of the company. Because of this, a log is necessary.

First of all, there may be a log to go with each piece of word processing equipment that uses paper tape or magnetic media. Take, for example, a Magna II, manufactured by A. B. Dick Company. This machine uses a magnetic card for recording typewriting. The card is made of a material much like that used on an audio tape recorder. Because it is not possible to *see* what is contained on magnetic cards, it is necessary to control the material that has been typed and recorded. Hence one log might have a page for each numbered (or otherwise identified) card that is used. On the page for a particular card, the last entry would indicate what is contained on the card, such as "Budget Report, 1981– 82." A simple glance at this page of the log for that particular machine would tell you what is contained on that card. The log will also indicate whether the material is to be reused. You would, therefore, know that you could not use that card. If the material is no longer needed, the log will indicate this. Some word processing departments keep a paper copy of each project in a file so that a person who needs to play back the material on a card can do so easily by looking at what is called a *hard copy* of the project.

Another kind of log is used by the person supervising the word processing department. Based on work requests coming from various departments, a record is kept of work that is currently *in-house* —that is, waiting to be prepared and returned to the department requesting it. In this way, the supervisor can keep track of what needs to be typed and returned each day. A particularly long project may take several days to complete. From the log, the supervisor knows when the material is needed and how much time it will take to finish it. By assigning the work to a word processing clerk, often called a *correspondence secretary,* in plenty of time to get it done, the supervisor ensures that everything will be finished and delivered on time. If a work request comes in marked *Rush,* that notation is made in the log. A log is, therefore, only a means of keeping track of a lot of material in the department.

Some of the newer equipment used in word processing is capable of producing its own log. The page illustrated on page 124 was prepared on a CRT text-editing machine. The operator properly coded the information needed and the equipment printed out exactly what was recorded on the tape by paragraph and by communication title.

However the log is kept, it is important that it be kept up to date at all times. Important records can be destroyed easily when logs are not properly maintained. Keeping one or several logs up to date may well be one of your responsibilities as an office worker.

Data Processing

Computer technology has advanced to such a degree that small and large businesses alike are able to purchase and maintain computers of one sort or another. Such computers have made it necessary to file still

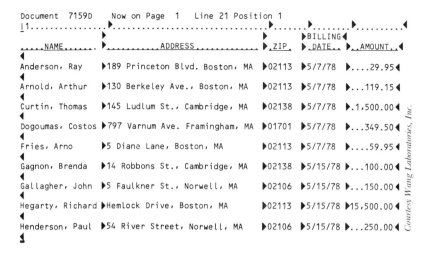

```
Document  7159D    Now on Page  1   Line 21 Position 1
|1..............▶.................................▶.......▶.......▶.........◀
                 ▶                               ▶      ▶BILLING◀
....NAME........ ▶...........ADDRESS............. ▶.ZIP. ▶.DATE.. ▶..AMOUNT..◀
◀
Anderson, Ray   ▶189 Princeton Blvd. Boston, MA  ▶02113 ▶5/7/78  ▶....29.95◀
◀
Arnold, Arthur  ▶130 Berkeley Ave., Boston, MA   ▶02113 ▶5/7/78  ▶...119.15◀
◀
Curtin, Thomas  ▶145 Ludlum St., Cambridge, MA   ▶02138 ▶5/7/78  ▶.1,500.00◀
◀
Dogoumas, Costos ▶797 Varnum Ave. Framingham, MA ▶01701 ▶5/7/78  ▶...349.50◀
◀
Fries, Arno     ▶5 Diane Lane, Boston, MA        ▶02113 ▶5/7/78  ▶....59.95◀
◀
Gagnon, Brenda  ▶14 Robbons St., Cambridge, MA   ▶02138 ▶5/15/78 ▶...100.00◀
◀
Gallagher, John ▶5 Faulkner St., Norwell, MA     ▶02106 ▶5/15/78 ▶...150.00◀
◀
Hegarty, Richard ▶Hemlock Drive, Boston, MA      ▶02113 ▶5/15/78 ▶15,500.00◀
◀
Henderson, Paul ▶54 River Street, Norwell, MA    ▶02106 ▶5/15/78 ▶...250.00◀
◀
```

Courtesy Wang Laboratories, Inc.

The first line of a printout from a text-editing machine shows the document number, page number, line number, and position on the line. The underscore below the last black triangle at the left indicates the position of the machine.

other types of media—punched cards, magnetic disk cartridges, and disk packs.

Instead of printed words and figures on paper, information is recorded in the form of punched holes or magnetic impulses. Cards, tapes, and disk packs must be stored for later use. The storage of such materials requires special equipment and supplies.

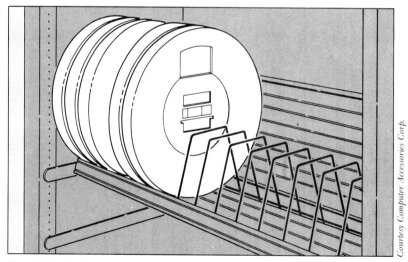

Courtesy Computer Accessories Corp.

Specially designed wire racks are used for storing magnetic disk cartridges.

Magnetic disk packs are stored efficiently on specially designed roll-out shelves.

Courtesy Computer Accessories Corp.

Micrographics

10.2 The increasing volume of paperwork in modern business offices has called for easier, more efficient methods of storing records that would permit records to be found with little effort and stored in minimal space. *Micrographics,* sometimes called microphotography, was developed in the early 1940s in response to the tremendous need for filing and retrieving intelligence information gathered during World War II. The aperture card was developed with the assistance of industry. A computer card, with a die-cut aperture in which the microfilm was hand mounted, was used to store the material. Because it was not necessary to have a paper copy of what was on film, and because the film could be viewed at the same size as the original or larger, it became a very efficient means of storing information. Roll microfilm was also used; this made the storing even more efficient. However, until technology provided for easy retrieval of records, viewing the records was more difficult.

Today, many companies manufacture equipment for recording information on microfilm, processing the film, and viewing records that have been filmed. Many of the readers, used for viewing, are also used as printers. Such readers can produce a paper copy of the record in its original size.

School systems keep permanent records on microfilm. Libraries from coast to coast film information from periodicals and other sources to provide easy access to this material. Banks and other businesses keep important records in less space by filming these records.

Microfilm is used in aperture cards, roll film, and sheets of microfiche. The equipment is as simple to operate as an office copier, and it is just as fast and efficient. Costs vary depending on the size of the documents to be filmed, the developing processes used, and the speed with which they are to be retrieved and viewed. If a company needs to film a great deal of material daily, it would be worthwhile to purchase a processor for their film. If time is not that important, and the amount of material is not too great, the company can send the material out to be filmed. The number of paper records needed and the frequency of their use generally determine whether a firm should purchase a reader or a reader-printer. Hence the nature of the business will dictate the amount and type of equipment purchased.

Estimates indicate that about 98 percent of the space normally used to store original records will be saved if the records are microfilmed. Microfilming cuts costs by reducing the space needed for files, reducing the number of files required, and reducing the labor needed to retrieve stored records.

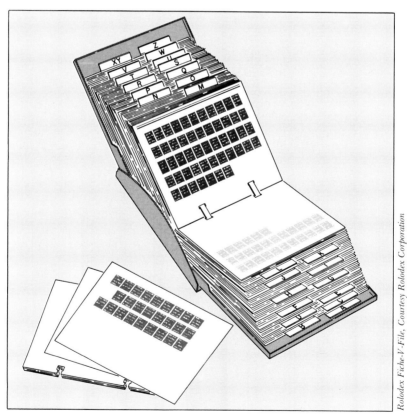

Rolodex Fiche-V-File, Courtesy Rolodex Corporation

Microfiche is easy to locate and is well protected in the clear plastic sleeves in this specially designed file.

Filmed records can be arranged in alphabetic order or according to any of the standard methods of filing. The outside of the box containing a reel of film indicates what is on the reel. The film file drawers or racks should also be labeled to help locate needed information.

Advantages of Commercial Systems

10.3 All the systems discussed so far have dealt with filing systems and procedures designed by businesses for their own use. It is often possible to set up a very efficient filing system. Unfortunately, however, many self-made systems soon reveal a lack of planning and become awkward to use and costly to maintain. For this reason, many manufacturers of filing equipment and supplies gladly provide the assistance of a filing consultant to aid executives, secretaries, or office managers in planning an efficient filing system. This specialist often recommends a ready-made *commercial system.* Commercial systems are based on the principles of alphabetic correspondence filing and are adaptable to any need.

Various features are available to speed up the filing and finding of material as well as to provide a double check against misfiling. These features include: (1) adding consistent color schemes to guide and folder tabs; (2) combining alphabetic and numeric coded captions; and (3) providing for special tab-position sections to take care of frequently used names.

Commercial systems often differ from one another in the arrangement of guides and folders as well as in some special features. They all include the following elements: (1) primary guides; (2) special guides, also known as secondary, or auxiliary, guides; (3) individual folders; and (4) miscellaneous folders. A *primary guide* is the main guide and always precedes the special guides, individual folders, and miscellaneous folders that are within the alphabetic range covered by the primary guide. Sets of primary guides may be obtained with from twenty-five to several thousand divisions of the alphabet. As the name implies, a *special guide* is used to show the location of records of a special nature that fall within the alphabetic range of the preceding primary guide.

Some patented systems are available from the manufacturers of filing equipment and supplies. That is, these systems are covered by a *patent,* which is an official document giving the inventor of the system the exclusive, or sole, right to the invention for a specific number of years. The patented system explained below is the Variadex System manufactured by Remington Rand. This description will illustrate some of the special features of a commercial system.

1. Primary guides have single captions and are placed in first position.
2. Miscellaneous folders are in second position and in *back* of the individual folders. They bear the same alphabetic caption as the primary guide.
3. Individual folders are in third position.

4. Special guides are in fourth position for names having a large volume of correspondence.

5. Special features: color is used on the guide tabs and on the folder tabs to speed up the location of records and as a check to prevent misfiling. The color of all folder tabs behind a guide is the same as the color of that guide tab. A worker would, therefore, be aware of misfiling if a folder with a green tab was placed with folders having blue tabs.

◆ HAVE YOU MET YOUR COMPETENCIES?

10.1 The following is a list of items to be logged in for word processing equipment. Prepare a log book page with the columns listed here: Date, Description, Originator, Machine, Operator, Due Date, Special Instructions. Record the documents on your log book page. (Use today's date.)

1. Mr. D. Long from the Transportation Department has requested a three-page report to be prepared on a magnetic typewriter. He will need it in four working days.

2. Ms. Osterhous has a ten-page manuscript to be typed on a magnetic-card typewriter. She will need it by this time next week.

3. A rush order from Miss Jane Engle requires one page of typewritten material that will not need to be revised later. She needs it today, if possible.

4. Mr. Ewald requests that an offset master of a single-page agenda be typed for his sales meeting, which is two working days away. (An offset master needs to be prepared on a carbon-ribbon typewriter.)

5. Jack Denzin would like a letter prepared for eighteen different people. The letter is the same for each person. The salutation and inside address will change. He needs these letters dated two days from now and they will be due to him on that date.

10.2 From the ten types of business records listed below, determine which of these are likely to be placed on microfilm.

bank statements	school permanent records
architectural drawings	employment applications
orders from customers	invoices
homework papers from students	checks
legal documents	parts catalogs

10.3 State the advantages of commercial systems in filing.

Note: If you are using the *Progress Filing Practice Set*, complete Job 55 (Final Test).

Glossary

Abbreviation. A shortened form of a word. In indexing, an abbreviation is considered as though it were spelled out.

Active file. A file cabinet reserved for records that are used frequently.

Address file. A card file containing frequently used names and addresses. Usually kept in a box or on a rotary wheel.

Alphabetic arrangement. The listing of names or topics in sequence according to the alphabet. This is called alphabetizing.

Alphabetic filing. Any system in which the captions are names of people, organizations, or letters of the alphabet.

Alphabetic subject filing. A filing system in which subject headings and divisions are alphabetized.

Alphabetize. To arrange in sequence according to the letters of the alphabet.

Cabinet. A container with one or more drawers for storing filed records.

Calendar pad. A number of sheets of paper, usually twelve, that includes one for each month of the year, stacked and glued together at one end. Each sheet includes boxes for each day of the month in which notations can be made regarding activities for that day.

Caption. A name, letter, or number under which records are filed.

Card filing. The processing and storing of business information on cards. There are two kinds of card files: vertical and visible.

Card index. A list that identifies assigned numbers in a numeric correspondence filing system. (See illustration on page 108.)

Carrier folder. A folder, usually of a distinctive color and made of a strong material, that is used to transport records.

Charge method. A procedure used to account for records that have been removed from the files.

Charging out. The procedure used to request and account for records removed from the files.

Chronological. In sequence according to date. When records are filed chronologically, the latest date is usually in front.

Classifying. Arranging in groups according to a predetermined plan.

Coding. The process of marking correspondence with the caption under which it will be stored.

Combination subject file. A method used when the volume of correspondence to be grouped by subject is small in comparison with records to be filed under the name of the person or organization. Subject captions are combined with name captions in one file.

Commercial system. A set of ready-made guides and folders manufactured for immediate use.

Compound geographic name. The name of a city, state, or other geographical location that includes more than one word.

Consecutive numeric system. The most commonly used numeric system. In this system, numbers are used consecutively, or in order. For example, 101 precedes 102, which precedes 103.

Consultant. One who gives professional advice concerning the operation and maintenance of files and records.

Contraction. A shortened form of a word made by omitting letters and drawing the shortened form together. An example is *don't.*

Correspondence. Any records in business, such as letters, telegrams, orders, invoices, bills, checks, reports, and miscellaneous papers, that are on sheets of paper and not on cards.

Correspondence book. A chronological record of outgoing correspondence made by typing an extra carbon of correspondence and placing these carbon copies in a loose-leaf notebook with the most current document in front.

Cross-reference. A notation in a file or an index showing that the record being sought is stored elsewhere.

Cut. The size of the tab on the back flap of a folder, usually expressed in a fraction. One-half cut, for example, means that the tab takes up one half of the back flap of a folder.

Cycle method. *See* Two-period transfer.

Data filing. *See* Subject filing.

Data processing. A term coined by the computer industry that indicates a system in which information is used, produced, and maintained by electronic computers.

Decimal-numeric system. A numeric filing system used when headings are subdivided more than twice. (See illustration on page 80.)

Degree. An educational title, such as Ed.D., that is conferred for certain advanced studies. Degrees are not filing units when they precede the full name of an individual.

Desk tray. A container for incoming or outgoing correspondence that is kept on office desks.

Desk-drawer file. A large file drawer contained in the desk. (See illustration on page 89.)

Dictionary arrangement. A subject arrangement of records used in smaller businesses and where division of topics is not needed. (See illustration on page 78.)

Disposing, disposition. The destroying or eliminating of records that are no longer needed.

Document. A paper containing information.

Double capacity. *See* Two-period transfer.

Double, or closed, caption. A caption that indicates not only where the section of the file starts but also where it ends.

Drawer. The part of a file cabinet that contains records.

Duplex-numeric system. A type of numeric filing system used when there are more than ten main headings or more than nine divisions or subdivisions under the same heading. (See illustration on page 80.)

Encyclopedic arrangement. An arrangement for a subject file in which the main categories are divided and subdivided. Generally used by large companies. (See illustration on page 78.)

Equipment. The cabinets, furniture, and miscellaneous devices used in handling and storing records.

Expansion. Any increase in the amount of equipment and supplies to permit the storing of more records.

Expansion score. Creases along the base of a file folder for later folding when more space is needed within the folder.

File. A container for storing records—a cabinet, open shelf, box, or any other type of housing.

File card. A cardboard slip used in both vertical and visible files.

File worker. An employee whose specialized job is to inspect, index, code, sort, and store records and to remove them from the files when they are needed.

Filing. The process of classifying, arranging, and storing records so that they can be obtained quickly when needed.

Filing period. The time during which records remain in the active files.

Filing shelf. A shelf that is attached to the front or the side of a file drawer to hold records during filing and finding operations.

Filing system. An arrangement of equipment and supplies to permit the storing of records according to a definite plan.

Film-reading machine. A machine used to view information that has been photographed on microfilm.

Finding. Locating a record that has been stored in a file.

Folder. A Manila container that holds correspondence in files.

Follower or compressor. A movable support that expands or contracts the usable space within a file drawer.

Follow-up. Checking on borrowed records to effect their return to the files.

Follow-up file. A file that calls attention to either (1) charged out records or (2) an office job that requires action on a certain date. It is usually arranged chronologically.

Follow-up folder. A folder with dates along the top edge that is clearly marked with a signal indicating when the records within the folder require action.

Forms file. A method of storing numerous types of forms for the most efficient use.

Freedom of Information Act. A law that allows people to see information kept on file about themselves.

Geographic filing. The alphabetic arrangement of records by location.

Given name. An individual's first name.

Guide. A sheet of heavy cardboard with a tab and caption used to guide the eye to the section desired in a file drawer. A guide also serves as a support for the records in the drawer.

Guide rod. A metal rod included in most file drawers that is placed through the guide rod extension in the bottom of the guides to hold them in place within the file drawer.

Guide rod extension. A projection at the bottom center of a guide that contains a metal-reinforced hole in the middle through which a guide rod is placed within the file drawer.

HFA file. Another name for a tickler file. The initials stand for "hold for action."

Hyphenated name. An individual or firm name that consists of words or letters connected by a hyphen. Both a hyphenated surname and a hyphenated firm name are considered as one unit for indexing.

"In," "out," and "hold" baskets. Containers kept on office desks and used for incoming work and business activities.

Inactive records. Records not subject to frequent use that are stored in less accessible and less costly equipment than active records.

Index card records. Any card file containing information. The cards may be in a drawer, in a box, on a rotary wheel, or in other special equipment. The size of the cards varies.

Indexing. The selecting of the caption under which a record is to be filed.

Indexing arrangement. The order in which the units of a name are considered for filing.

Individual folder. A folder that contains records concerning only one correspondent or subject.

Inspecting. Checking correspondence for a release mark before storing.

Label. A sticker that is attached to the tab of a guide or a folder and on which the caption appears.

Letterhead. Stationery with a printed heading.

Log book. A notebook containing records of important business transactions. A log book may be used to record incoming and outgoing mail, telephone calls, or other business transactions.

Main numeric file. The primary file in a system using numbers. This file contains individual folders that are placed behind the appropriate guide. Inside these folders, records are maintained in chronological order with the most recent record in front.

Maximum-minimum transfer. A plan for periodically transferring records from active to transfer files. A maximum and a minimum period of time is set for storing records in the active files.

Microfilming. The photographing of records at greatly reduced size on filmstrips, cards, or rolls. The film can be maintained in only two percent of the space required for the original records.

Miscellaneous alphabetic file. The part of a numeric file used for those correspondents for whom sufficient records have not accumulated to merit a number being assigned to them.

Miscellaneous folder. A folder that contains records for correspondents or subjects not active enough to warrant an individual folder.

Misfiling. The storing of a record in a location other than where it should be.

Multiple transfer. *See* Two-period transfer.

Numeric correspondence file. A filing system organized in three parts: a main numeric file, a miscellaneous alphabetic file, and a card index in which the names of correspondents or subjects are arranged alphabetically.

Numeric filing. The filing of correspondence or cards according to number.

Numeric subject file. A basic kind of subject file that includes several systems that use numbers for captions in place of words. (See illustration on page 79.)

One-period transfer. A plan in which the active files contain records for the current filing period only. At stated intervals all the records are transferred.

Open-shelf filing. A method of filing in which shelves, rather than filing cabinets with drawers, are used to store records.

Out folder. A folder used to store correspondence while the regular folder is out of the files. It indicates that the regular folder has been borrowed from the files.

Out guide. A guide used to indicate that a folder has been borrowed from the files.

Periodic transfer. The removal of records at stated intervals from the current active files to the inactive transfer equipment.

Perpetual transfer. The constant transfer of records from the current to the inactive files.

Political division. An area created by law, such as a town, city, county, state, or country.

Position. The location of a guide or folder tab from the left to the right of the file drawer.

Possessive. A word indicating ownership that usually contains an apostrophe. In indexing, the letter *s* after the apostrophe is considered.

Posted card records. Card files that are used to record new information on a continuous basis.

Prefix. A word element, such as *Mc*, at the beginning of a word or name.

Preposition. A word used to connect a noun or a pronoun with some other word. In indexing, prepositions such as *for, in,* and *of* are disregarded.

Primary guide. The main guide for a section of filed records.

Privacy Act. A law that allows individuals to designate which people may see records and information kept on file about themselves.

Punched cards or tape. Cards or tape in which holes are punched for purposes of recording information.

Records. All written information that is used by an organization whether it is in the form of correspondence, cards, tapes, or microfilm.

Records management. The planning, organizing, and controlling of the creation, protection, use, storage, and disposition of records.

Reference. The directing of an individual's attention to a source of information.

Register. A list of correspondents and the numbers assigned to them in a numeric correspondence file.

Relative index. An alphabetic list of all the headings and subheadings in a subject file.

Release marks. A notation showing that the record has received the required attention and is ready for filing.

Requisition slip. A form used to request records from the files.

Retention. A period of time during which records are kept in either active or transfer files before they are destroyed.

Retrieval. Finding—the major goal of any filing system.

Sequence. A logical order, either according to the letters of the alphabet or numbers.

Signal. A plastic, metal, or paper device used to guide the eye to pertinent information. Usually in card and visible files.

Single caption. A caption that indicates only where the section of the file starts. Only one letter or one combination of letters appears.

Sorting. The arranging of records in sequence after they have been coded to facilitate storing.

Soundex. A commercial numeric filing system that brings together in the files all names that sound alike but may be spelled differently.

Staggered arrangement. The placing of guide or folder tabs in successive positions from left to right in the file drawer.

Storing. The placing of records in a file container.

Subject filing. The alphabetic arrangement of records by names of topics or things.

Substitution card. A card used to replace a single record that has been removed from a file folder. This card indicates the name of the borrower.

Summary. A record of the business transactions that take place while an employer is away from the office.

Supervisor. The person who is responsible for the operation and maintenance of files and filing systems.

Surname. The last name of an individual.

Surname prefix. The part of a surname that precedes the body of the surname, such as *Del, Fitz, Mac, O',* and *Von.* Prefixes are indexed as part of the surname.

Suspense file. Another name for a tickler file.

Tab. A projection above the body of guides and folders on which the caption appears.

Terminal-digit filing. A numeric arrangement of records according to the last, rather than the first, digits.

Tickler file. A follow-up file, usually organized by date.

Time stamp. The notation on an incoming piece of correspondence to indicate the date and, often, the hour of receipt.

Title. A word indicating rank, office, or privilege. A title is considered an indexing unit only when it precedes a single name or when it appears in a firm name.

Topical filing. *See* Subject filing.

Transfer. The removal of records from the active files to inactive files.

Transfer file or box. A container that stores transferred records. This container is usually made of inexpensive cardboard or metal materials.

Transpose. To rearrange the normal order of a name.

Two-period transfer. A plan in which the active files provide space for current records and records from the last filing period. At transfer time only the oldest records are removed.

Unit. Each part of a name used in indexing.

Vertical filing. The storage of records on edge.

Visible filing. The storage of cards in specially designed equipment so that the information near the edges of the cards can be seen easily.

Word processing. A means of processing written information within an organization by using special automated typewriters for fast, efficient production.

Word processing log. A log book kept in the word processing department in which a record is made of all incoming work. Logs are also kept for information that is recorded on magnetic media for various machines.

Index

Abbreviations, indexing of, 30
Active file, 81; *illus.,* 83
Address files, 22
Addresses, indexing of, 34
Alphabetic filing, 5, 46
  advantages and disadvantages of, 46
  arrangement of guides and folders in,
      47–51, 52; *illus.,* 53
  captions for, 48; *illus.,* 48
  indexing for (*see* Indexing rules)
  labels for, 51
  subject (*see* Subject filing)
Alphabetizing, 10
Answer sheet, *illus.,* 15, 22
Article "the," indexing of, 29
Articles, conjunctions, and prepositions,
    indexing of, 29

Banks and other financial institutions,
    indexing of, 35–36

Cabinets, 52
  efficient use of, 52
  location of, 97–98
  selection of, 97–98, 99
  transfer, 81–84
Captions, 48
  alphabetic, 48; *illus.,* 48
  geographic, *illus.,* 115
  numeric, *illus.,* 108
  subject, *illus.,* 76
Card files, 22–26; *illus.,* 23, 24, 26
  advantages of, 22
  alphabetic (*see* Indexing rules)
  cards for
    selection of, 22
    typing of, 25; *illus.,* 26
  date, 95; *illus.,* 96
  follow-up, 95–96
  index card records, 22
  purposes of, 22
  vertical, 24; *illus.,* 24
  visible, 25; *illus.,* 26
Card index
  alphabetic (*see* Indexing rules)
  alphabetic subject, 77
  geographic, 115
  numeric, 106; *illus.,* 106
  numeric subject, 79
  rotary visible, *illus.,* 23
Carrier folders, 63
Charge-out system, 62

Charging out
  follow-up, 65
    folders for, 64; *illus.,* 64
  forms for, *illus.,* 63
  handling of requests, 62
  need for, 62
  steps in, 62
Chronological arrangement, 51
Coding, 59; *illus.,* 50
Combination subject file, *illus.,* 76
Conjunctions, indexing of, 29
Consecutive numeric filing, 104; *illus.,*
    105
Control system (*see* Charge-out system)
Correspondence
  coding of, 59; *illus.,* 58
  definition of, 46
  filing of (*see* Filing)
  handling of, 56
  indexing of, 59
  sorting of, 60; *illus.,* 58
Correspondence books, 91
Creating a new file folder, 66
Cross-referencing, 20, 40
  in geographic filing, 116; *illus.,* 116
  in numeric filing, 109
  in subject filing, 73; *illus.,* 74

Data processing, filing and, 123
Date files, 95
Date stamp (*see* Time stamp)
Decimal-numeric system, 80
Degrees, indexing of, 17
Desk, items on, 91
Desk, reference materials on, 92
Desk calendar pad, 95
Desk-drawer file, 88
Dictionary arrangement, 77; *illus.,* 78
Double (or closed) captions, 48
Duplex-numeric system, 80

Educational institutions, indexing of, 36
Encyclopedic arrangement, 77; *illus.,* 78
Expansion score, 50

Federal government names, indexing of,
    37
File drawers
  capacity of, 47
  efficient use of, 47
  overcrowding of, 47

Filing
  basic methods of (*see also each method*),
    5
  card (*see* Card files)
  choice of systems, 5–6
  definition of, 2
  design of system, 97–100
  job entry-level skills, 2
  office occupations, 2
  steps in, 57
  steps preliminary to, 56
Firm names, indexing of, 28–34
Folders
  arrangement of (*see each filing method*),
    52; *illus.*, 53
  capacity of, 50–51
  carrier, 63
  follow-up, 95, 111
  hanging, 49
  individual, 50
  labels, typing of, 51
  miscellaneous, 51
  out, 63; *illus.*, 64
  overcrowding of, 50–51
  scoring of, 50
  selection of, 49
  storing in (*see* Storing)
Follow-up
  card, 95
  folders for, 96; *illus.*, 97
Foreign government names, indexing
  of, 38
Forms file, 89
Freedom of Information Act, 7

Geographic filing
  advantages and disadvantages of, 114
  arrangement of guides and folders in,
    114; *illus.*, 115
  captions for, *illus.*, 115
  card index for, 115
  cross-referencing in, 116; *illus.*, 116
  steps in, 117
Government names, indexing of, 37–38
  federal government, 37
  foreign government, 38
  state and local government, 37
Guides
  arrangement of (*see each filing method*)
  captions on, 48; *illus.*, 47, 48
  designs of; *illus.*, 47
  number required, 47
  out, 63; *illus.*, 64
  selection of, 47
  staggered, 49; *illus.*, 49
  tabs on, 47
  typing of labels on, 51
Guide rod, 47
Guide rod extension, 53

Handling paperwork, 93
Hanging folders, 49

HFA ("hold for action") file, 95
Hospitals and religious institutions, indexing of, 36
Hotels and motels, indexing of, 36
Hyphenated names, indexing of,
  firm names, 30
  individual names, 16

"In," "out," and "hold" baskets, 88
Inactive file, 81; *illus.*, 83
Indexing rules
  abbreviated names of individuals, 17
  abbreviations in firm names, 30
  addresses, 34
  alphabetic order, 11
  articles, conjunctions, and preposi-
    tions, 29
  banks and other financial institutions,
    35
  educational institutions, 36
  federal government names, 37
  first word first, 28
  foreign government names, 38
  hospitals and religious institutions, 36
  hotels and motels, 36
  hyphenated names, firms, 30
  hyphenated names, individuals, 16
  last name first, 12
  nothing comes before something, 11
  numbers, 32
  one or two words, 31
  parts of geographic names, 33
  possessives and contractions, 31
  prefixes, 15
  seniority terms and other designa-
    tions, 17
  single letters, 30
  state and local government, 37
  titles, 16
Individual folders, 49, 50–51
Individual names, indexing of, 11–20
Inspection of correspondence, 57, 58;
  illus., 58

Labels
  alphabetic, *illus.*, 53
  file drawers, *illus.*, 61
  folder, 48
    attaching and typing of, 51–52
  geographic, *illus.*, 115
  guide, 47
  selection of, 51
  subject, *illus.*, 74
Lateral files, 52
Log books, 90
Lost records, search for, 67–68; *illus.*,
  68

Magnetic cards and tapes, 123, 124
Main numeric file, 106; *illus.*, 108
Married women, indexing names of, 16
Micrographics, 125

Miscellaneous alphabetic file, 107; *illus.,* 108
Miscellaneous folders, 51

Names, indexing of (*see* Indexing rules)
Numbers, indexing of, 32
Numeric correspondence file, 106–109
Numeric filing
  advantages and disadvantages of, 104
  arrangement of guides and folders in, 107
  card index for, 108; *illus.,* 108
  consecutive-numeric, 104; *illus.,* 105
  cross-referencing in, 109; *illus.,* 109
  main file for, 108; *illus.,* 108
  miscellaneous alphabetic file for, 107; *illus.,* 108
  register for, 106; *illus.,* 106
  steps in, 109; *illus.,* 108
  subject (*see* Subject filing)
  terminal-digit, 105; *illus.,* 105
  uses of, 104

Office occupations, filing and, 2
Organization of supplies, 92
Out folders and guides, 65; *illus.,* 64

Parts of geographic names, indexing of, 33
Pending file, 95
Periodic and perpetual transfer, 81 (*see also* Transfer)
Possessives and contractions, indexing of, 31
Posted card records, 22
Prefixes in surnames, indexing of, 15
Prepositions, indexing of, 29
Pressboard transfer file, *illus.,* 84
Privacy Act, 7
Punched cards and tapes, 124

Records
  categories of, 81
  control of, need for, 62
  as factor in choice of filing system, 57
  lost, search for, 67–68; *illus.,* 68
  organization of (*see each system*)
Register, numeric file, 106; *illus.,* 106
Relative index, 77, 79
Release marks, 56; *illus.,* 58
Reminder system (*see* Tickler file)
Requisition card, *illus.,* 63
Retrieval, 80, 100
Rotary visible card index, *illus.,* 23
Routing slip, 64–65

Seniority terms, indexing of, 17
Single captions, 48

Sorting, 57, 58, 60, 75; *illus.,* 75
Staggered arrangement, 49
State and local government names, indexing of, 37
Storing, 57, 58, 60; *illus.,* 61
  procedures for efficient, 60
Street addresses, indexing of, 34
Subject filing
  advantages and disadvantages of, 72–73
  alphabetic, 75; *illus.,* 76
  arrangement of guides and folders in, *illus.,* 76
  captions for; *illus.,* 76
  combination, 75; *illus.,* 76
  cross-referencing in; *illus.,* 74
  dictionary arrangement in, 77; *illus.,* 78
  encyclopedic arrangement in, 77; *illus.,* 78
  nature of, 72–73
  numeric
    card index for, 106
    decimal-, 80; *illus.,* 80
    duplex-, 80; *illus.,* 80
    simple-, 79, 80
  organization of, 106
  reasons for use of, 72
  steps in, 73; *illus.,* 75
Substitution cards, 65; *illus.,* 64
Summary, 93
Surname prefixes, indexing of, 15
Suspense file, 95

Tabs, cuts and positions of, 48; *illus.,* 48
Terminal-digit system, 105; *illus.,* 105
"The," indexing of, 29
Tickler file, 95; *illus.,* 96
Time stamp, 56; *illus.,* 57
Titles, indexing of, 16
Transfer
  microfilming as factor in, 126
  need for, 81
  periodic plans of, 81
    maximum-minimum, 82
    one-period, 82
    two-period, 82
  perpetual, 81
  planning for, 84; *illus.,* 84
  savings gained by, 81

Unit, definition of, 10

Vertical filing (*see* Filing)
Visible card files, 25; *illus.,* 26

Word processing, 3, 122–123
Word processing log, 122